Start Canoeing

Start Canoeing

ANNE WILLIAMS

Illustrated by Debbie Piercey

Stanley Paul

London Melbourne Sydney Auckland Wellington Johannesburg

Stanley Paul & Co. Ltd

An imprint of the Hutchinson Publishing Group

3 Fitzroy Square, London W1P 6JD

Hutchinson Group (Australia) Pty Ltd
30–32 Cremorne Street, Richmond South, Victoria 3121
PO Box 151, Broadway, New South Wales 2007

Hutchinson Group (NZ) Ltd
32–34 View Road, PO Box 40–086, Glenfield, Auckland 10

Hutchinson Group (SA) (Pty) Ltd
PO Box 337, Bergvlei 2012, South Africa

First published 1980

Set in Linotron Rockwell

Printed and bound
in Great Britain by
Redwood Burn Limited
Trowbridge & Esher

ISBN 0 09 141500 4 cased
      0 09 141501 2 paper

Frontispiece: *Richmond Falls, 1977* (William G. Sampson)

Contents

Acknowledgements

To Oliver Cock, whose enthusiasm for
canoeing is boundless, my sincere thanks for
reading the manuscript and for writing the
Foreword. To Rosemary Edmonds, my first
canoeing companion, for typing the
manuscript. To David Howard, for supplying
information about canoeing in the USA, and
to Valley Canoe products. To Ian Brown of the
PE Department of Dundee University, for his
interest and assistance, and to all those with
whom I have canoed.

Lastly, I thank my husband, Bryan for his
constructive criticism and my daughter Katy,
for her forbearance. The responsibility for
the contents and any omissions therefrom
remains, of course, my own.

Photographs by Anne Williams,
Chris Hawkesworth and William G. Sampson.

Foreword

I first met Anne Williams when she came to a meeting of slalomists at Bisham Abbey National Sports Centre near Marlow on the Thames in Buckinghamshire. It was a very technical conference, divided into two halves, one for those less practised in the sport and one for the specialists. I remember that an Admiral was so flummoxed by the technical jargon in the specialist section that he moved down into the beginners group; but Anne was at a physical education college and stayed most firmly with the experts.

It was my first meeting with Anne, it was very far from the last. She competed in slaloms and marathon races but her heart was really in the expedition side of canoeing; touring, and in particular sea-touring. She taught canoeing; firstly in schools and later for a long spell at the National Mountaineering Centre in North Wales. Here she rose to be head of the department for canoeing and she was teaching at all levels of the sport, particularly on the recreational side, both inland on rivers and lakes and on the sea.

I think that the students who found themselves in her hands were the luckiest ever; they could not have found a better instructor. Highly knowledgeable in her sport, extremely able to impart her knowledge, adventurous yet safe (a very difficult combination to achieve) and always forceful yet patient in getting the students to achieve the goals she had set them, Anne was one of the best Coaches of the British Canoe Union.

Oliver J. Cock, MBE
Director of Coaching 1962–78
British Canoe Union

Chapter One
Introduction to Canoeing

It is seven o'clock. The weather is grey and misty with little wind. It could develop into a fine day. A last check of the gear, fill the flasks, telephone the coastguard and drive to the coast. There is a long, smooth swell breaking on the shore as we change and pack the canoes. The mist is lifting and we can see something of the big cliffs of the coastline we have come to explore. From our study of the chart we expect some interesting canoeing in the tide race between the mainland and a group of offshore islands. There is also known to be a variety of sea birds and a colony of seals living on the cliffs and in the caves. We launch the canoes and paddle away in anticipation of a good day.

Sea canoeing. Just one of the many branches of an exciting sport. We could just as easily be setting off on a demanding day down a wild-water river, a leisurely paddle on canal or lake or a fortnight's holiday on rivers or sea. Whatever your inclination, age, sex or physical fitness canoeing has something to offer you.

Historical background

Canoes are probably the oldest and most versatile form of water transport known to man. Those we use to-day have evolved from two basic types, the birch bark canoes of the North American Indians and the Arctic skin boats of the Eskimo.

The birch bark canoe, an open boat, was designed for one or more people, kneeling and using single-bladed paddles. It was mainly used for transporting people and possessions up and down big rivers. The Eskimo kayak, a decked-in boat, was usually designed for one person, sitting and using a double-bladed paddle. It was mainly used for hunting.

The history and development of canoeing is fascinating and the relevant books mentioned in the book list make good reading.

The eskimo kayak

Left: *Sea canoeing*

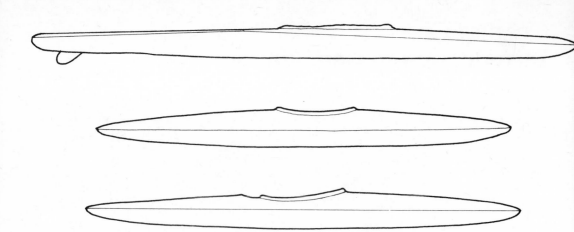

Above: *The KI sprint (top), the slalom (middle) and touring canoe (bottom)*

Below: *A calm coast – sea canoeing at its most peaceful*

Basic design

This is a book about paddling modern versions of the Eskimo kayak, variously called canoeing or kayaking depending on where you live. The kayak has been successfully adapted to meet the varying demands of the many types of water on which it is possible to canoe. Some of these designs will be very sophisticated and produce boats suitable for one specific purpose. Others will be a compromise of design and may be used for several types of canoeing.

A very general guide is that a long, narrow canoe with a long waterline length, will go fast in straight lines. A shorter canoe, with a short waterline length, more width (or beam) and a curve from front to back along the bottom (rocker) will be slow in straight lines but turn easily

More specific details of design appear in the section 'What next?'

Buying a canoe

Do not buy a canoe of your own until you have some experience of canoeing. You will almost certainly regret your choice, as a canoe which satisfies the novice may be technically outgrown in a period of weeks. Instead, try to borrow or hire a canoe until you know which type of canoeing you prefer. One way is to join a local canoe club where canoes can be borrowed and where you may also be able to buy a second-hand boat. Buying a second-hand boat can be a risk and if you are not able to buy through a club, do take along someone who can recognize major defects before you buy. The majority of kayaks are currently made in glass-reinforced plastic (GRP) and are easily repaired (see page 170). However, if the canoe has had hard use, particularly in competitive slalom, there may be stress fractures not easily detected by the inexperienced.

Buying a new canoe is expensive but provided you go to a reputable firm, there will be no other problems. In Britain the British Canoe Manufacturers Association safeguards standards (see page 170). Do be quite sure what type of canoeing you are going to do before you buy.

How to learn to canoe

Residential courses

Probably the quickest way to get a lot of canoeing experience is to attend a residential course, school or holiday which specializes in canoeing. You will work through all the basic techniques and the concentrated practice will give you a sound start. It is also an excellent opportunity to try out a variety of canoes before buying your own.

Non-residential courses

Many local or national bodies, educational establishments and youth clubs will run canoeing sessions in the summer evenings and at weekends. These are well worth attending and have the advantage of being local to you.

Canoe clubs

Your local canoe club will be pleased to welcome you. Informal instruction will be offered. You will meet canoeists from your own area and you will be able to buy second-hand gear, share club transport and boat storage facilities.

With friends

If your friends are canoeists you have an ideal opportunity to learn with them.

Alone

Generally speaking, it is unwise to canoe alone, especially as a beginner. It is a slow and potentially dangerous process.

If you like the general idea of a club, then it is certainly worth joining your local canoe club, possibly following a short instructional course. If not, you may prefer the idea of a concentrated course which would enable you to canoe with friends.

The following chapters should speed up your learning process and show you some of the potential of modern kayaks.

Chapter Two
Clothing and Equipment

Clothing

If you are lucky enough to live and canoe in a hot country where the water is always warm then the choice of clothing is simple. For those who live in colder climates and where weather conditions change rapidly proper insulation is vital.

Conventional clothing provides insulation by trapping air, which is a relatively poor conductor of heat. Several thin layers of clothing trap more layers of air and will be more efficient than one thick layer. Provided this air remains still and dry, the body will stay warm. This is illustrated by such people as the Lapp, Eskimo, Sherpa, Andean Indian and others who, adequately insulated, can live and work at exceedingly low temperatures. Wind soon lowers the temperature to an uncomfortable level by disturbing the layers of air. This can largely be counteracted by wearing a windproof anorak and overtrousers.

Waterproof clothing will cause increased sweating and condensation which will make the clothing underneath wet. If you fall in the water, the clothing underneath will also become wet. In both cases the insulation of the trapped air will be lost, if you keep on the wet clothing and the waterproofs, having first climbed out of the water in the latter case, and continue to do physical work, you will soon warm up inside the waterproofs.

More specialized clothing is available to provide insulation during and after immersion, some of which is suitable for canoeing. Even in summer, the surface water of the sea round North America, Northern Europe and Britain is rarely more than 20°C., which is far too cold for long periods of immersion and could prove fatal in as little as six hours to anyone wearing conventional clothing. Salt water is usually at least 4° warmer than fresh water.

A well equipped canoeist (Chris Hawkesworth)

It is certainly worth the extra expense of buying good clothing, but do not do so until you have done a little canoeing and also had a chance to observe other canoeists. The following illustrations will help you make a choice. Remember it is almost always colder afloat than ashore.

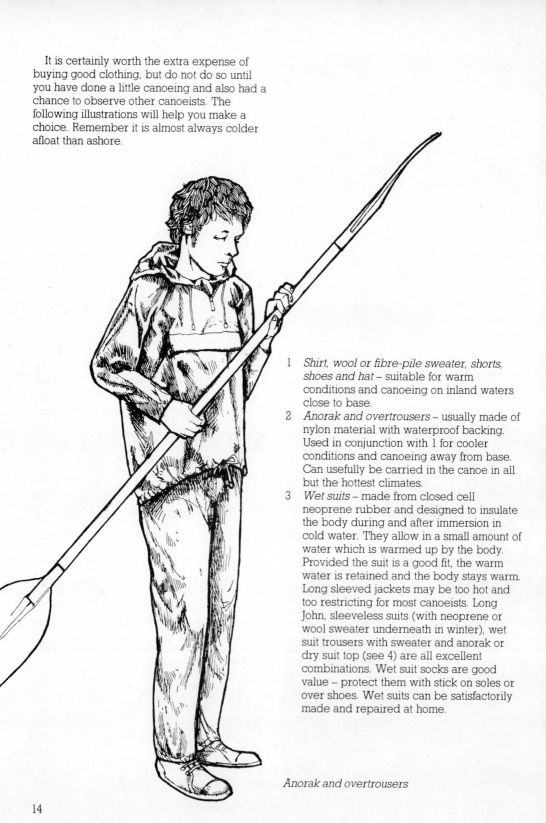

1 *Shirt, wool or fibre-pile sweater, shorts, shoes and hat* – suitable for warm conditions and canoeing on inland waters close to base.
2 *Anorak and overtrousers* – usually made of nylon material with waterproof backing. Used in conjunction with 1 for cooler conditions and canoeing away from base. Can usefully be carried in the canoe in all but the hottest climates.
3 *Wet suits* – made from closed cell neoprene rubber and designed to insulate the body during and after immersion in cold water. They allow in a small amount of water which is warmed up by the body. Provided the suit is a good fit, the warm water is retained and the body stays warm. Long sleeved jackets may be too hot and too restricting for most canoeists. Long John, sleeveless suits (with neoprene or wool sweater underneath in winter), wet suit trousers with sweater and anorak or dry suit top (see 4) are all excellent combinations. Wet suit socks are good value – protect them with stick on soles or over shoes. Wet suits can be satisfactorily made and repaired at home.

Anorak and overtrousers

4 *Drysuits* – made of thin rubber, are worn over conventional clothing. They rely on a tight seal at neck, wrists and ankles, the top and bottom of the suit rolls together at the waist to form a waterproof seal. Excess air must be expelled as the suit is put on to avoid risk of it collecting in the legs in the event of a capsize. These suits provide excellent insulation by keeping the conventional clothing dry and retaining the trapped air insulation. They are easily torn and once damaged lose their effectiveness. They can be bought ready made or made and repaired at home from a kit.

5 *Fibre pile sweater and trousers* – this man-made, usually nylon, fabric provides insulation in the normal way, by trapping air. It is very comfortable to wear and dries more quickly than cotton or wool. It loses its insulation when immersed in water for long enough to force out the trapped air.

6 *Canoe anorak* – specially designed for the canoeist. Made of nylon with neoprene waterproofing. Several designs with or without hood and neoprene cuffs. Gives good protection when worn over wool or fibre-pile sweater and with wet suit trousers.

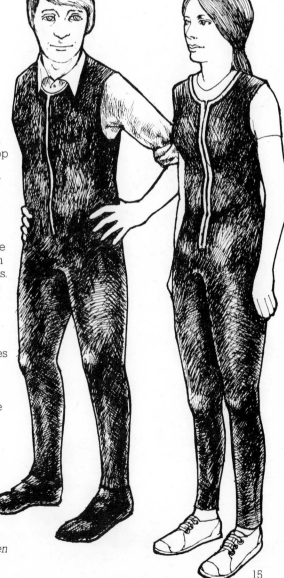

Wetsuits for men and women

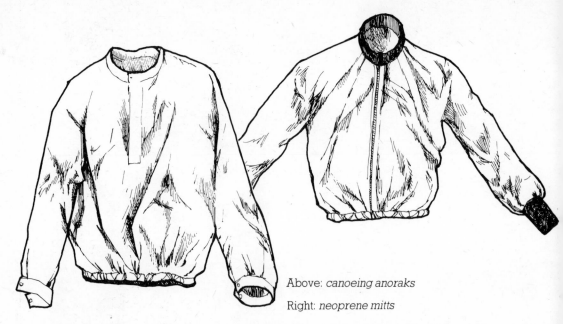

Above: *canoeing anoraks*

Right: *neoprene mitts*

Below: *correct and incorrect footwear*

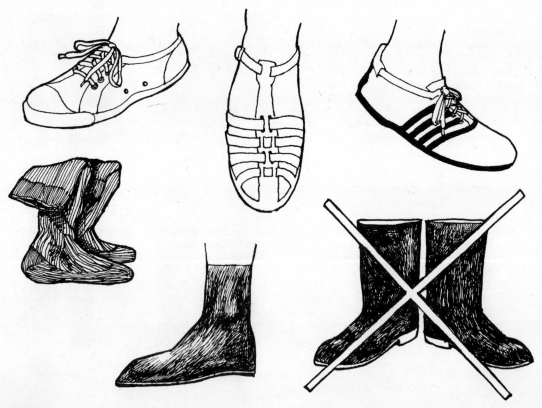

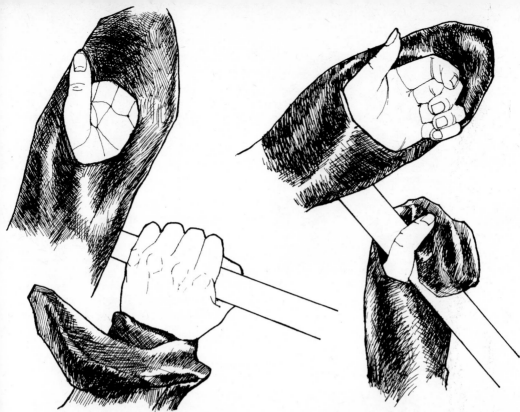

7 *Footwear* – it is essential to wear some sort of shoes as you may have to wade in rock strewn rivers or launch over beaches and rocks. Choose plastic sandals or canvas rubber-soled shoes. Woollen, fibre-pile or wet suit socks can provide extra insulation. Avoid heavy footwear, such as boots, which might impede swimming.

8 *Gloves* – it is very difficult to find a satisfactory answer to the problem of cold hands. Most types of gloves impair the control of the paddle, but some people do wear wet suit gloves. Open palm neoprene mitts can be useful as they are easy to roll back quickly when not required. They are easy to make at home from odd pieces of neoprene.

9 *Hats and helmets* – the head is particularly vulnerable to hot sun and cold, wet, windy conditions, so choose a shady or warm hat as required. Helmets are needed for wild water rivers, surfing and coastal trips. They are specially designed in plastic or GRP, the latter being rather heavy to wear. Most will have adjustable cradles inside for accurate fitting and good drainage holes. Choose a design that covers the ears and comes well down over the forehead.

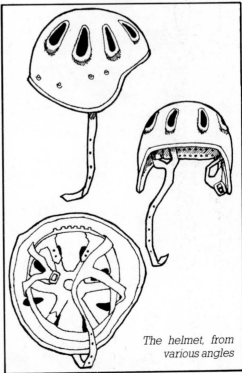

The helmet, from various angles

The canoe and gear for a day out

Now that you have some idea of what is available, choose whatever clothing suits you and your pocket and the type of canoeing you intend to do. Remember that the head and the trunk contain the vital organs of your body and insulate them properly.

Orange, yellow and dayglo red are the colours most easily seen in the water, so it is worth buying or making your outer clothing in these colours.

Life-saving jackets and buoyancy aids

To avoid drowning is an essential feature of canoeing! You should learn to swim before starting canoeing, but even then, personal buoyancy should be worn by all canoeists. There are various types of buoyancy available and they fall into two categories:

1   *Life-saving jacket* – designed to cope with the very worst situation – that of supporting an unconscious person in rough water. It must turn the person on to their back within

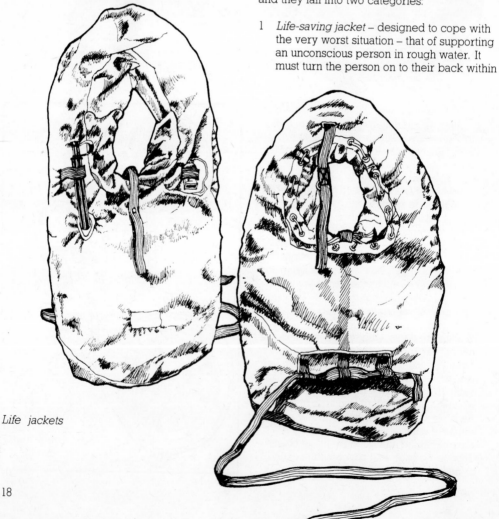

Life jackets

three seconds, turn them to face oncoming waves, support them with face clear of the waves, protect vital nerves in the neck, and remain firmly in position throughout. To do this requires 35 lb, or 16 kg of buoyancy which produces a large, uncomfortable garment. Lifejackets are available which have 13½ lb or 6 kg of inherent buoyancy, are comfortable to wear, enable the canoeist to get out of a capsized canoe easily and can then be inflated by mouth to the full 35 lb or 16 kg. For beginners, those canoeing on exposed waters and those who ultimately choose to canoe alone, a lifesaving jacket is recommended. In the United Kingdom this jacket will conform to the British Standards Institution Specification 3595.

2 *Buoyancy aids* – many varieties available. Those which rely entirely on inflation are vulnerable to damage and should be avoided. Choose instead one of the closed cell foam types designed for the canoeist. Some of these jackets can be bought with a life-saving inflatable jacket carried in a special pocket for use when heavy conditions occur.

Worn properly, a life jacket will float the body face upwards

It will turn the wearer to face oncoming waves

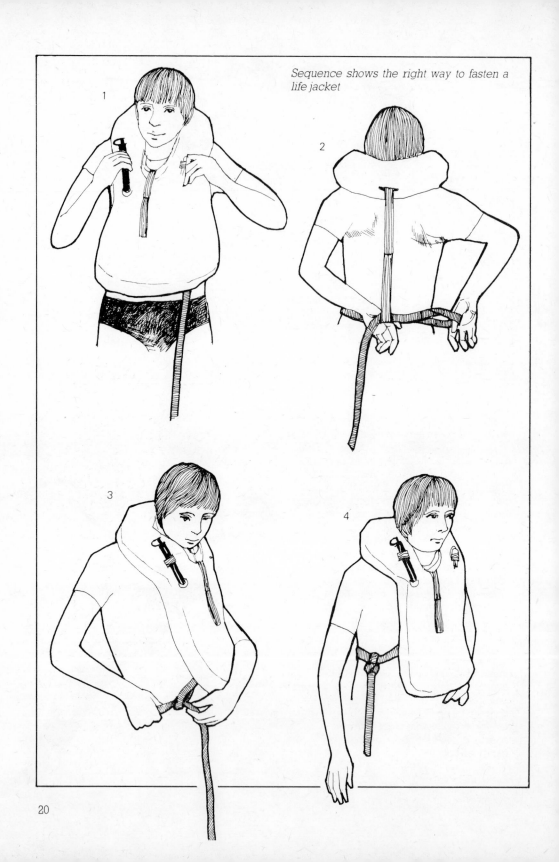

Sequence shows the right way to fasten a life jacket

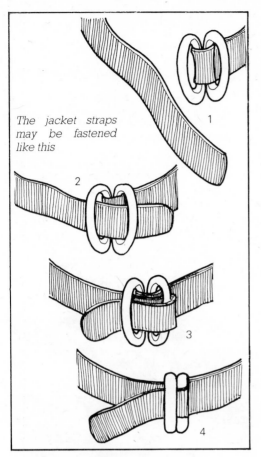

The jacket straps may be fastened like this

Choose a lifejacket or buoyancy aid to suit your needs and then wear it. Orange, yellow or fluorescent colours are preferable. Make sure that the jacket is adjusted to fit you and that all fastenings are correctly secured. Small children have a different centre of gravity from adults and must have a jacket designed for their size and weight. People wearing wet suits and some physically handicapped people will also have a different centre of gravity which may counteract some of the advantages of a lifejacket and make a buoyancy aid more suitable.

If you wish eventually to take part in competition, buy a jacket that conforms to the International Canoe Federation regulations, (minimum buoyancy of 13½ lb or 6 kg). In the United States of America it is recommended that you buy a jacket approved by the U S Coastguard and in Britain by the Ship and Boat Builders' National Federation which give manufacturing guarantees.

Recommended buoyancy aids

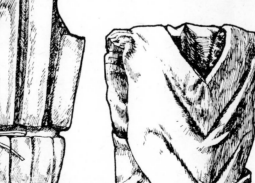

Spraydecks

An apron-like garment worn round the waist which fits over the cockpit rim to keep out water and keep in a certain amount of heat. It should be long enough to come well up the body with an adjustable or elastic top (a); if the top tends to slip down and allow water in, add a pair of braces (b). The apron part should be taut to shed water quickly. The lower edge should fit over the cockpit rim with elastic. A quick release strap should be securely sewn to the underside of the deck so that the elastic is released from the rim before the weight of the pull comes on to the stitches.

Spraydecks are most commonly made of nylon fabric with polyurethane or neoprene waterproofing, the latter being more flexible and longer lasting. They are also and more expensively made in neoprene foam rubber. This gives an excellent fit and sheds water quickly. It is easily damaged, so protect with a standard spray deck. The neoprene decks can also be bought with a vest-shaped top, fastening over the shoulders with velcro tabs (c); this gives added insulation and is an efficient way of keeping out the water. The top can be rolled down when not required.

Canoe buoyancy

The majority of canoes currently in use are made of glass reinforced plastic (GRP) and if filled with water, they will sink. Therefore, you should fill the canoe you use with buoyancy only leaving room for yourself and your gear. Bought canoes will have some built-in buoyancy, usually polystyrene blocks which also act as additional deck strengtheners. Check these regularly to see that they are firmly in place and add as much additional buoyancy as you can. Air bags are suitable for this as they can be inflated to fill all the space. Extra polystyrene blocks, if available, can be cut to fit. Whatever system you use, fasten it in well and check frequently.

Spraydecks give protection and conserve heat

Footrests

These consist of flanges on the inside of the hull through which are bolted the ends of a metal bar. This can be adjusted forwards or backwards to suit the leg length of the canoeist (b). The flanges and fittings must be able to stand great impact, especially if you are surfing or river canoeing when your weight could be transferred rapidly on to the footrest. It is wise to back up the footrest with a polystyrene block in case the flanges or bar should fail (c). Some footrests, called fail-safe, are fixed at one end only, the other end slides into a bolt-on fitting on the opposite flange which holds the footrest firmly against your feet, but allows it to swing towards you. If in surf or other heavy water your feet should be forced beyond the footrest, it would be fairly easy for you to withdraw them, using your feet to pivot the footrest towards you (d).

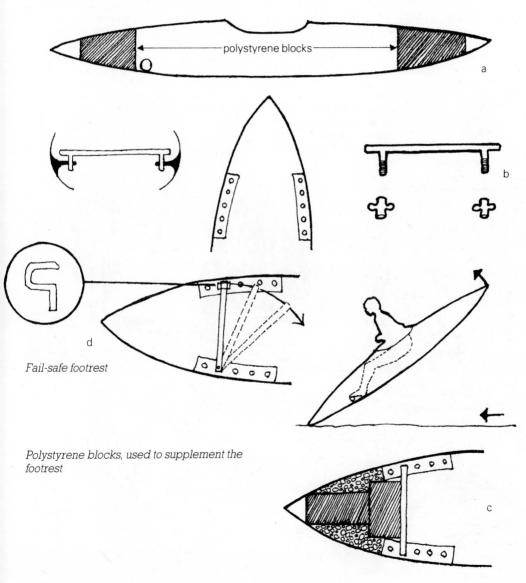

polystyrene blocks

a

b

d

Fail-safe footrest

Polystyrene blocks, used to supplement the footrest

c

Waterproof containers

From the beginning of your canoeing career, you will need to carry food, clothing and other equipment in your canoe. You must pack the gear in suitable containers which must be strong, fit into the canoe through the cockpit or hatch, remain there by being tied in or otherwise secured, and above all, remain waterproof. There are many ways of doing this, depending on how much money you want to spend.

1 Cheap and efficient are heavy gauge polythene bags. Use two bags per package as the outer bag may get damaged.
(a) Fill the bag only two-thirds full, hold the empty part and flatten it well.
(b and c) Carefully pleat this part.
(d and e) Fold pleated part twice.
(f) Tie tightly or use rubber bands cut from car tyre inner tube. Put the bag inside another bag and repeat the process.

2 Purchase or make a tubular shaped bag of waterproof material. Seams must be welded or taped, to be waterproof. Use a polythene bag inside for extra safety and fasten both as in 1.
3 Use rigid polythene containers. These can sometimes be bought from canoe outfitters, but many good quality domestic containers are available from general stores. Increase water-proofness by taping on the lids of those you seldom open (e.g. first aid, emergency food/clothes) with waterproof tape or use a collar of neoprene foam rubber or car inner tube.
4 Purchase from canoe stockist rubberized fabric bags. These are excellent but expensive so protect them inside another bag. They are easy to fasten with a multi-fold top secured with press studs. Also inflate to give added buoyancy and insurance against loss. Come in all sizes, including camera bag.

The way to pack in polythene bags

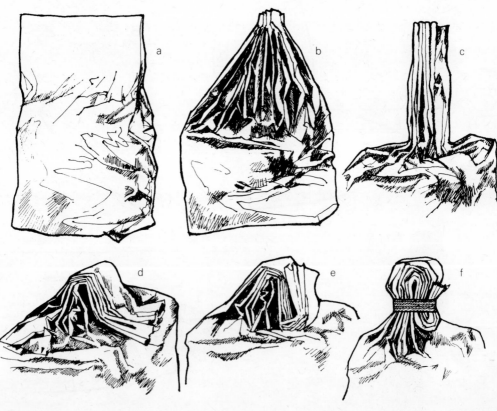

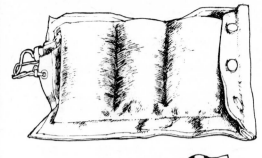

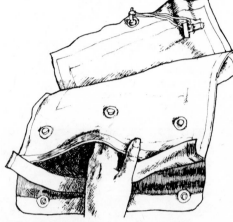

Rubberized fabric bag

Whatever system you choose, each container must fit into the canoe. You may find that a combination of different types gives the best result.

Paddles

During the initial learning period you do not need a sophisticated paddle, but do need to find out whether you are left- or right-handed for canoeing (see page 40) and what type of paddle you ultimately require. If you can borrow or hire equipment to start with, you may save money in the long term. If not, buy a simple paddle or paddle kit consisting of two plywood blades or plastic blades which are pushed into a plastic-covered alloy tube. This shaft or loom can be shortened as required, which makes it an ideal paddle to buy for children. The blades are set at right angles to each other and held with a retaining screw. As the blades are flat, not curved, it can be used by left- or right-hand control paddlers. These blades will see you through your first season and some people choose always to paddle with flat blades. If you do decide to buy a pair of curved blades, the flat ones will easily convert into 'split' paddles, to carry as spares in your canoe.

Right-handed, left-handed and flat-blade paddles

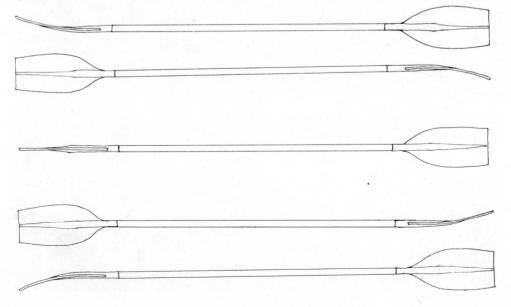

Types available

Apart from the flat-bladed paddles already mentioned, there are many makes of paddle available. Good paddles are expensive but well worth the money in terms of feel and efficiency. Most are made of wood or fibreglass or a combination of these two.

1 *Wood* – made of laminations of hard and soft woods, tipped with metal. The loom is oval for grip orientation and strength. The blades are curved along their length and some may also be curved across their width, or spoon-shaped. Wooden paddles are the most expensive. You must specify the overall length and left- or right-hand control when purchasing (see page 25).

2 *Fibreglass (GRP)* – made in a variety of ways which means there is a wide price range. Some are all fibreglass, some will have alloy or wood looms and fibreglass blades. Wooden shafts have the advantage of the oval shape. The blades may be curved or spooned and again you must specify overall length and left- or right-hand control when purchasing.

Good paddles are vital to the canoeist. Use the flat blades for a season until you know if you are left- or right-hand control and the length and type of paddle you need.

Wild-water racer (left) *and K2 marathon canoe*

Car roof rack

For carrying two or three canoes safely on a car roof, you are strongly advised to buy a roof rack designed for the job. The extra leverage exerted by the canoes, especially in windy conditions, is great. Normal luggage racks have only two points of attachment and are rarely safe. The canoe or dinghy type is in two separate halves so that the attachment points are as far apart as possible. The rack must be securely fitted to manufacturers' instructions and frequent checks made on the bolts. The canoes should be tied on with suitable rope and not elastic cords which sometimes fail. Also tie together the ends of the canoes and secure to front and back of the car.

Trailers

If more than three canoes are to be transported regularly, a trailer should be considered. With the right facilities available it is possible to build a suitable trailer or convert an existing one. Several canoe manufacturers will supply trailers and trailer firms are usually willing to convert a standard model to your requirements, which could include a box for paddles, gear etc. Contact a reputable stockist, preferably near your home so that you can liaise over details.

All good equipment is expensive. Unless you are very lucky, you will not be able to buy all you need at once. Rather buy a good lifejacket and anorak initially and add the other items gradually as you can afford them.

Carrying canoes on a roof rack

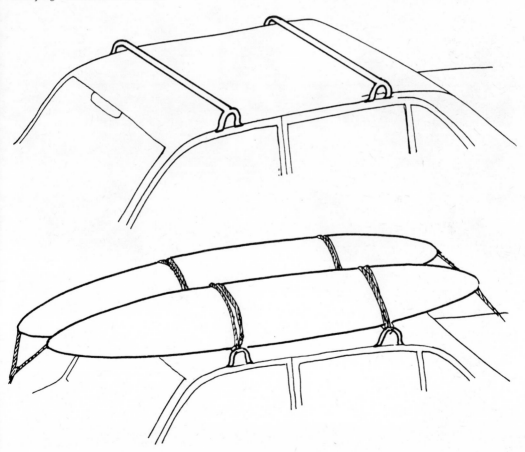

Chapter Three
Basic Techniques

Learning to canoe should be fun. You will probably waste effort initially worrying about falling in the water. Start your canoeing when the water is relatively warm and try to relax and enjoy your surroundings. You may not capsize at all until you become more adventurous and anyway, if you are to become a canoeist you will fall in the water countless times and think nothing of it. Windy conditions make the learning process more difficult, so find calm and sheltered water for your first attempt.

Left: *Adjusting spraydecks*

Below: *Decklines. Bow loop and toggle*

Carrying the canoe

If two people are available, each cups one hand under the opposite ends of the canoe, or use the toggles found on some canoes. Avoid lifting by the deck lines which are not designed for that purpose.

Most single canoes, unladen, can be carried by one person:

1   Stand beside the cockpit. Crouch down and roll the canoe on to its side, cockpit towards you.
2   Slide one arm inside the cockpit and as you lift the canoe on to your shoulder, stand up. Balance the canoe with the free hand and, once you feel confident, carry your paddle.
3   When you get to the water's edge, lower the canoe to the ground.

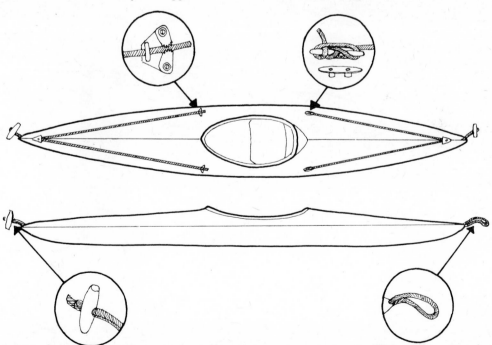

The way to lift and carry a canoe

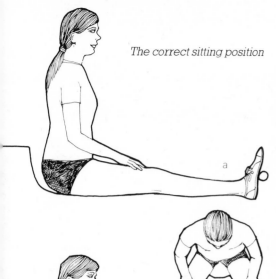

The correct sitting position

Adjust the footrest

Adjust the footrest so that when you are sitting back in the seat and leaning slightly forward from the waist, your legs straight, your insteps rest against the footrest (a). In this position you cannot paddle satisfactorily but you can rest your legs when not working and so avoid discomfort. To paddle the canoe, draw your knees up and push them firmly under the deck on each side. Press your toes down on to the footrest. You will now have contact with the canoe with your seat, knees and feet which will help you to control the canoe (b).

Put on your spray deck and buoyancy aid or lifejacket and place your paddle within easy reach.

Launching and embarking in shallow water

1 Pick up the canoe by the cockpit, holding the paddle also, walk into the water to about mid-calf depth.
2 Lower the canoe into the water. It will float lower in the water with you in it, so check the depth and look for rocks underneath. Now get in!

Launching in shallow water

Lower the canoe into the water

There are many ways of doing this, and that most suitable for beginners is first described here. It will feel awkward at first but you will quickly learn which method suits you best. Keep your centre of gravity low and only lean on the mid-line of the canoe.

1 Stand beside your canoe facing the front. Put one end of your paddle on the deck immediately in front of the cockpit and the other end, blade flat on the ground at right angles to the canoe (a).

a

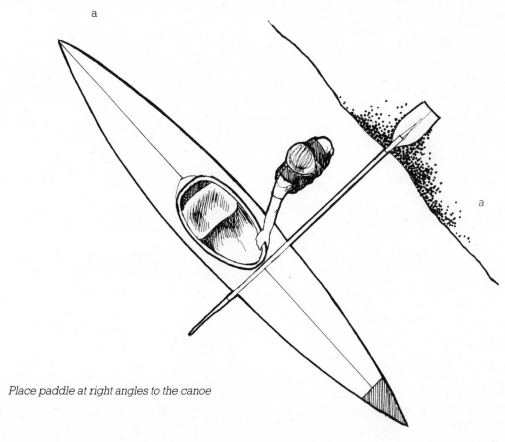

a

Place paddle at right angles to the canoe

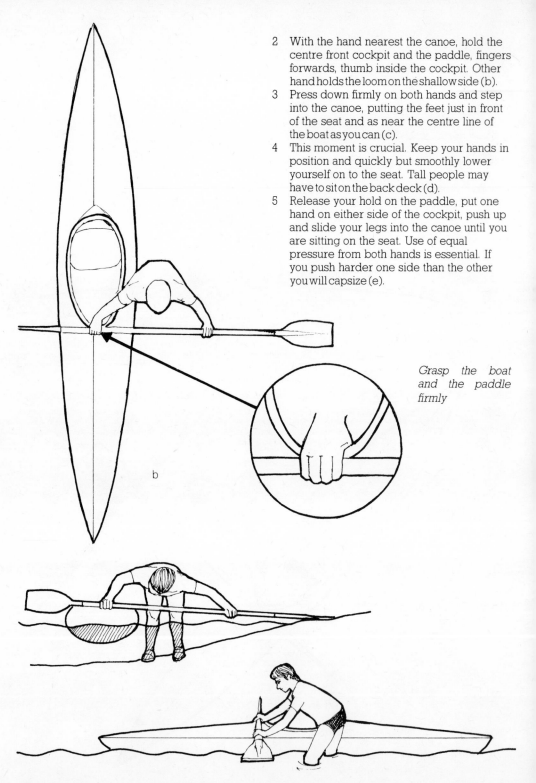

2 With the hand nearest the canoe, hold the centre front cockpit and the paddle, fingers forwards, thumb inside the cockpit. Other hand holds the loom on the shallow side (b).
3 Press down firmly on both hands and step into the canoe, putting the feet just in front of the seat and as near the centre line of the boat as you can (c).
4 This moment is crucial. Keep your hands in position and quickly but smoothly lower yourself on to the seat. Tall people may have to sit on the back deck (d).
5 Release your hold on the paddle, put one hand on either side of the cockpit, push up and slide your legs into the canoe until you are sitting on the seat. Use of equal pressure from both hands is essential. If you push harder one side than the other you will capsize (e).

Grasp the boat and the paddle firmly

b

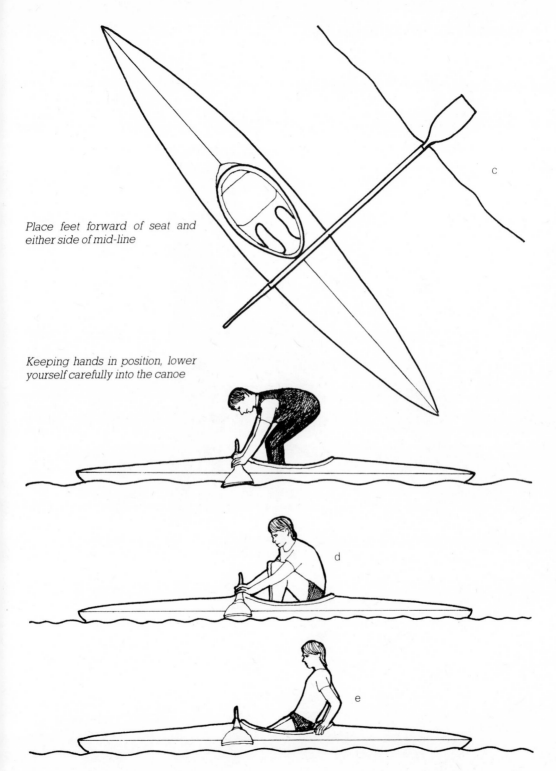

Place feet forward of seat and either side of mid-line

c

Keeping hands in position, lower yourself carefully into the canoe

d

e

Launching and embarking into deep water

If the bank or shore drops steeply into the water, carry your canoe to the edge.

Lower one end on to the water and push the canoe away from you until the whole canoe floats. Keep a firm hold on the painter or deck line and swing the canoe parallel to the bank.

Preparing to launch in deep water

Now embark as before; that is:

1 Paddle across front deck and on to bank.
2 Face front of canoe, hand nearest canoe grasps centre of cockpit and paddle shaft. Other hand grasps shaft over the bank.
3 Press down on both hands, step into canoe.
4 Lower yourself on to back deck or seat.
5 Move both hands to sides of cockpit to adjust position.

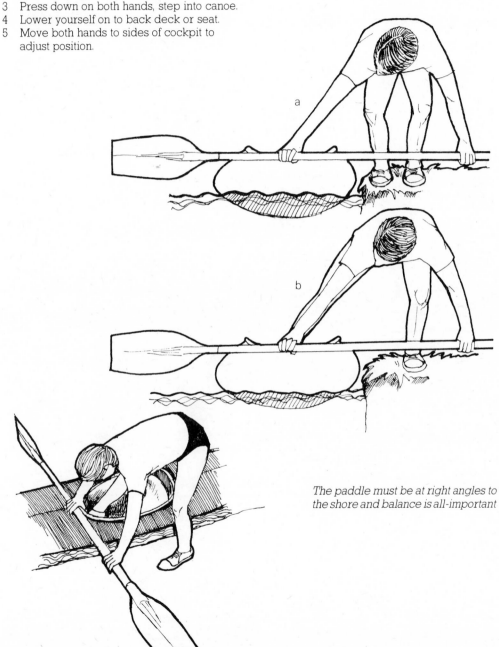

The paddle must be at right angles to the shore and balance is all-important

Alternative methods of embarking

As soon as you feel able, dispense with using the paddle to lean on as it can be damaged. Lie the paddle across the deck so that it is quickly available. Stand in the water beside the canoe, then:

1 Put one foot into the canoe and one hand on either side of the cockpit.
2 Lower yourself on to the seat.
3 Lift the second foot in.
4 Adjust your position.

If none of these methods suits you, this last one is very safe. It punishes the paddle but adapts to any situation.

1 Paddle lies across deck behind the cockpit. Other end on beach, shore, bank or rock.
2 Face front of canoe, standing or sitting in front of paddle shaft (a).
3 Hand nearest canoe grips paddle shaft and centre back of cockpit coaming. Fingers inside cockpit (b).
4 Other hand on shaft well out towards the bank (c).
5 Take your weight on your arms, sit on the shaft between your hands. Lean slightly towards the bank (d).
6 Put both feet into the canoe, in front of the seat.
7 Straighten your legs and lower yourself on to the seat.
8 Now move your hands.

Getting in without using the paddle

The safest way to embark, though hard on the paddle

Getting into a canoe needs practice. Basic points are the same whichever method you use:

1 Keep your centre of gravity low. That is, crouch or sit down, never stand up in the canoe.
2 Move smoothly and deliberately.
3 Place your feet in front of the seat and on either side of centre line of the boat.
4 Sit down as soon as you can. Keep your hands in position until you have sat down.
5 Only lean on centre front or centre back of cockpit, or on both sides equally.

Getting out

Getting out is exactly the reverse of getting in. Manoeuvre the canoe parallel to bank or shore-line so that you get out into shallow water, then:

1 Organize the paddle into position, either in front or behind the cockpit.
2 Place your hands in position as for getting in and take your weight on your arms.
3 Move your feet out of the canoe until you can sit or stand on the shore.
4 Hold on to the canoe and lift it clear of the water.

The paddle

The various types available are described on pages 25 and 26

Length

A very flexible guide is to stand beside the upright paddle and with your arm held above your head, cup your fingers over the end of the paddle. Different water requires different paddle lengths. Narrow, rocky rivers need short paddles. Long distance or sprint racing and touring need longer ones. Use the finger-tip guide until your personal preference dictates otherwise.

Left- or right-hand control

It is essential to establish whether you are a left- or right-handed canoeist. This may follow your usual bent but many left-handed people canoe with right-hand control and vice versa, so if, after a reasonable period of experimentation, the paddling action feels unnatural, try changing the control hand. Ultimately you must stick to one control hand as many canoeing skills depend on the degree of accuracy which this gives.

Flat bladed paddles can be used left- or right-handed, curved blades are specifically one or the other, so do not buy curved blades until you are sure of your control hand.

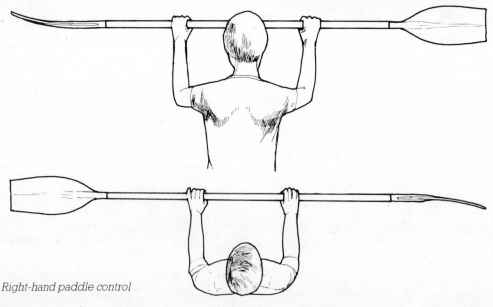

Right-hand paddle control

Right-hand control

Hold your paddle above your head, elbows bent to a right angle. Now lower your paddle into position in front of you, with the right blade vertical (if using a curved blade, concave side facing you) and ready to enter the water. The left blade will be horizontal concave side upwards (a).

From now on, hold the right hand firmly in place and do not allow it to slip round or along the shaft. The left hand holds the shaft but allows it to turn inside the hand.

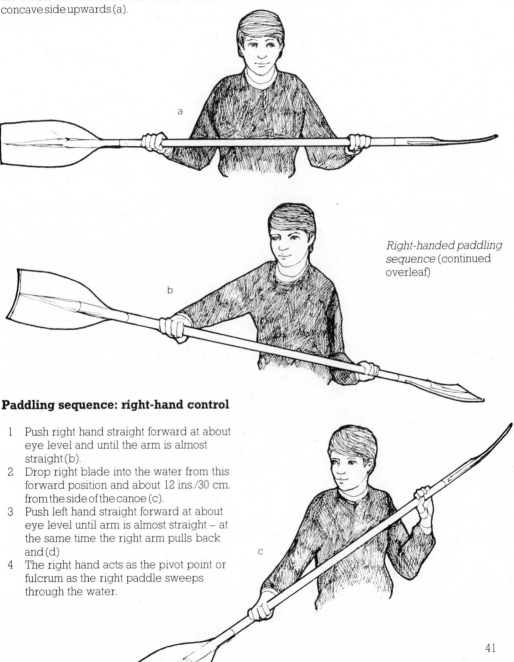

Right-handed paddling sequence (continued overleaf)

Paddling sequence: right-hand control

1 Push right hand straight forward at about eye level and until the arm is almost straight (b).
2 Drop right blade into the water from this forward position and about 12 ins./30 cm. from the side of the canoe (c).
3 Push left hand straight forward at about eye level until arm is almost straight – at the same time the right arm pulls back and (d)
4 The right hand acts as the pivot point or fulcrum as the right paddle sweeps through the water.

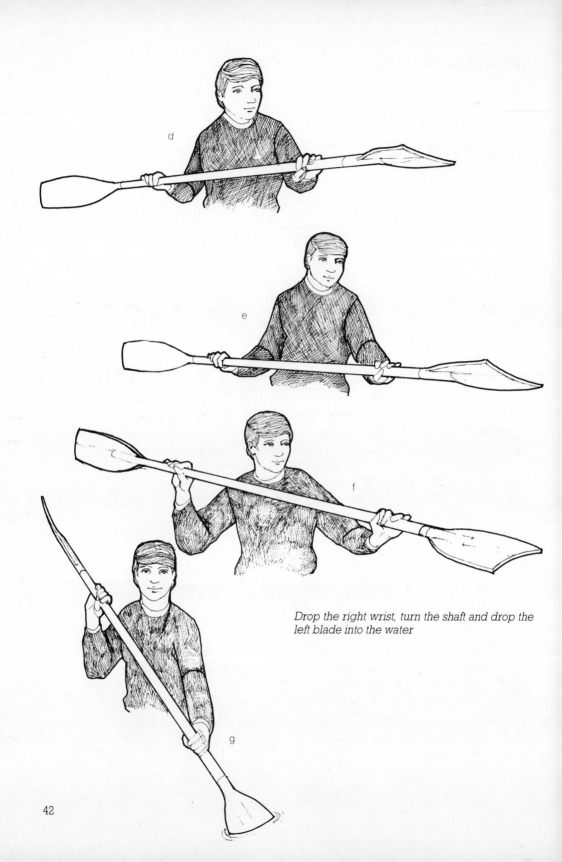

d

e

f

Drop the right wrist, turn the shaft and drop the
left blade into the water

g

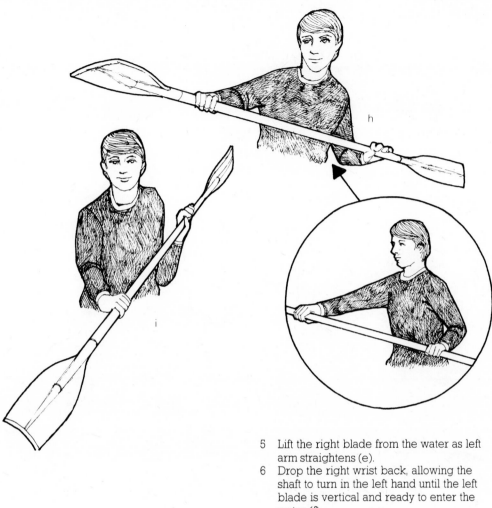

5 Lift the right blade from the water as left arm straightens (e).

6 Drop the right wrist back, allowing the shaft to turn in the left hand until the left blade is vertical and ready to enter the water (f).

7 Drop left blade into water from the forward position and about 12 ins./30 cm from side of canoe (g).

8 Push the right hand straight forward at about eye level until arm is almost straight – at the same time the left arm pulls back and (h)

9 The left hand acts as the fulcrum as the left paddle sweeps through the water.

10 Lift the left blade from the water as right arm straightens (i).

11 Repeat sequence.

Left-hand control

Hold your paddle over your head, elbows bent
in a right angle. Now lower your paddle into
position in front of you, knuckles uppermost,
with the left blade vertical (if using a curved
blade, concave side facing you) and ready to
enter the water. The right blade will be
horizontal (concave side uppermost). From
now on, hold the left hand firmly in place and
do not allow it to slip round or along the shaft.
The right hand holds the shaft but allows it to
turn inside the hand.

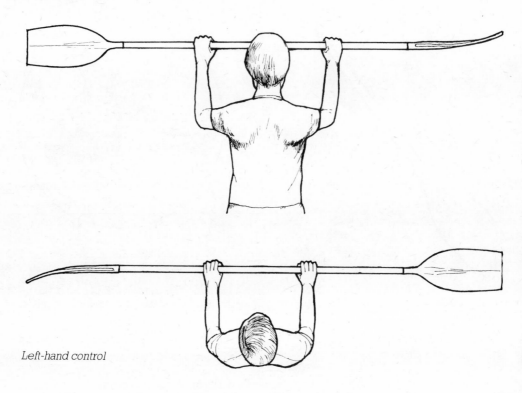

Left-hand control

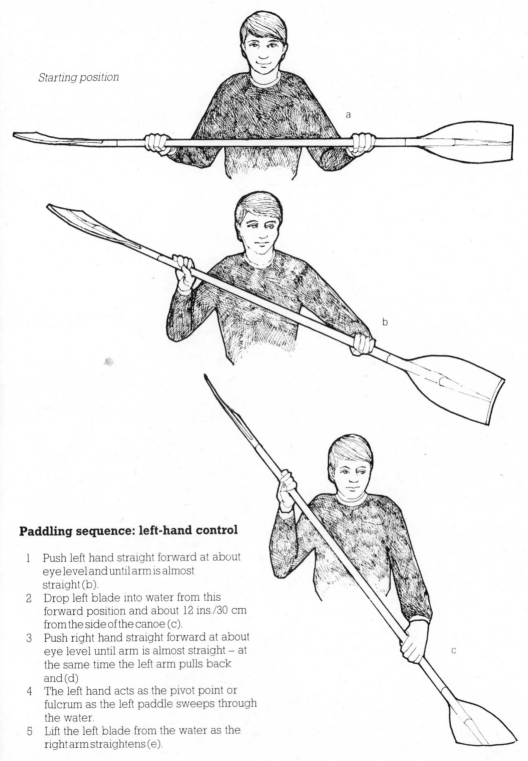

Starting position

a

b

Paddling sequence: left-hand control

1 Push left hand straight forward at about eye level and until arm is almost straight (b).
2 Drop left blade into water from this forward position and about 12 ins./30 cm from the side of the canoe (c).
3 Push right hand straight forward at about eye level until arm is almost straight – at the same time the left arm pulls back and (d)
4 The left hand acts as the pivot point or fulcrum as the left paddle sweeps through the water.
5 Lift the left blade from the water as the right arm straightens (e).

c

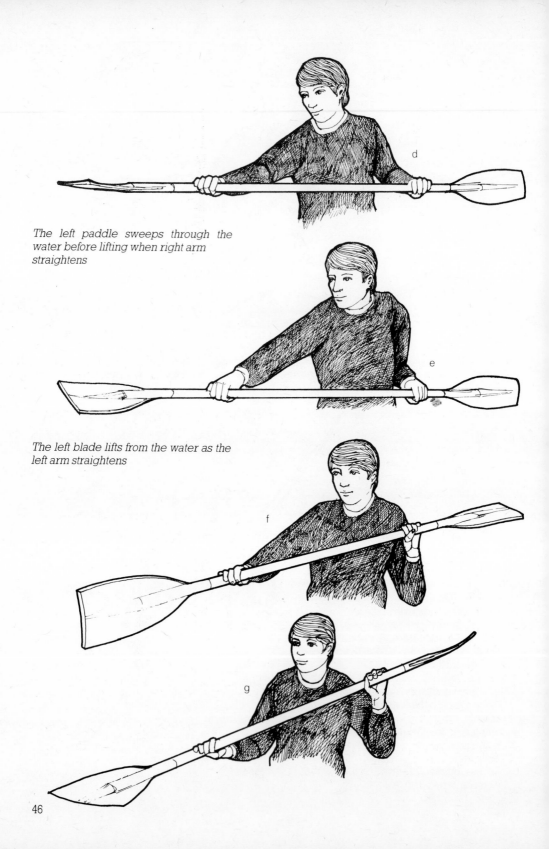

The left paddle sweeps through the water before lifting when right arm straightens

The left blade lifts from the water as the left arm straightens

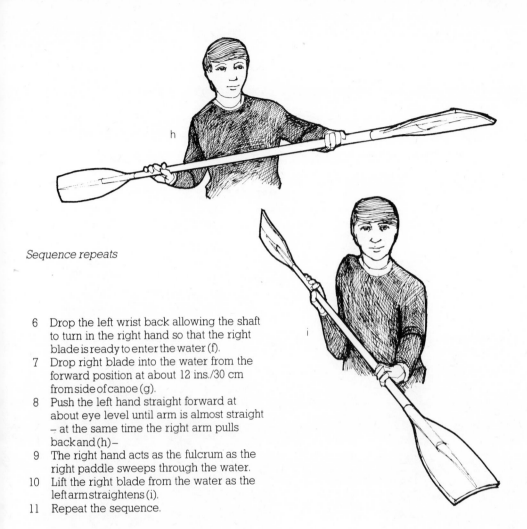

Sequence repeats

6 Drop the left wrist back allowing the shaft to turn in the right hand so that the right blade is ready to enter the water (f).
7 Drop right blade into the water from the forward position at about 12 ins./30 cm from side of canoe (g).
8 Push the left hand straight forward at about eye level until arm is almost straight – at the same time the right arm pulls back and (h) –
9 The right hand acts as the fulcrum as the right paddle sweeps through the water.
10 Lift the right blade from the water as the left arm straightens (i).
11 Repeat the sequence.

The main points to note in both right- and left-hand control are:

1 Lean forward and relax.
2 Paddle slowly.
3 Push the paddle through the water with the upper arm. This utilises the strong muscles of your back.
4 Use the lower hand as the fulcrum as the arm sweeps back.
5 Keep your control hand in position at all times. Drop the wrist back to adjust the angle of opposite blade.
6 Push the upper arm straight forward. Avoid allowing it to cross the centre line of canoe.
7 Take charge of the canoe with your legs as described on page 31.

Try paddling around for a while. Keep your body and hands relaxed and paddle slowly. If the canoe begins to go off course, be prepared to paddle more than once on the same side to correct it. Also, pick out an object on the shore to paddle towards rather than looking at the front of the canoe. Steering a straight course is a knack you will soon learn. The use of a sweep stroke, described later, will help you.

Be prepared to paddle more than once on the same side

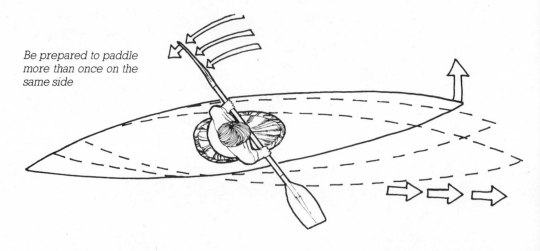

Paddle towards a stationary object

Try this exercise to show yourself just how much your legs contribute to your canoeing:

1   Sit in the canoe, knees under the deck ready to paddle.
2   Hold your paddle in both hands at shoulder height.
3   Keep your hands and paddle absolutely still throughout.
4   Gently lean your canoe to the right – support the canoe with your left knee. Right the canoe again by pushing your right knee up under the deck.
5   Repeat on the left.

Use of legs to control canoe

6   Speed up the process so that you rock the canoe vigorously from side to side. Each time, keep the paddle and upper body still and use the legs to control the angle of the canoe.

This is an excellent way of appreciating the degree of control you get from a well-fitting canoe. If you are going to canoe on moving water, sea or river, you must learn to lean your canoe over on its side to carry out efficient turns and support strokes. It is well worth spending time adjusting the footrest and adding extra padding to the footrest and seat to ensure that you have a secure base from which to work.

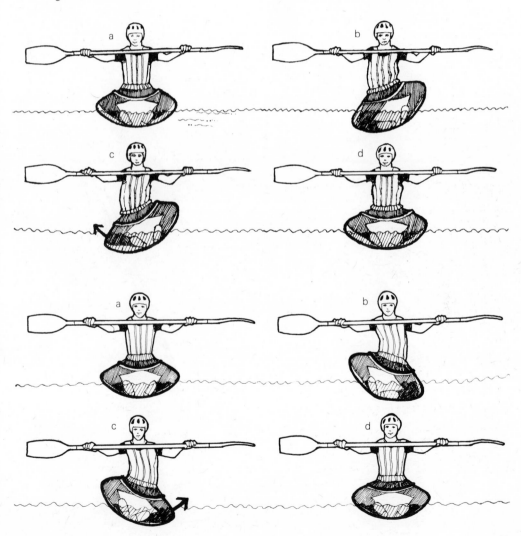

Reverse paddling

1 Check behind you that there is room to
move backwards – look behind you all the
time you are moving.
2 Use the back of the blade. Keep your
control hand in its normal position.
3 Turn the body from the waist so that you
can put the blade in the water well behind
you.
4 As in forward paddling use the upper arm
to lever with and the lower arm as the pivot
point.
5 Keep the paddle clear from the sides of the
canoe as it sweeps through the water.

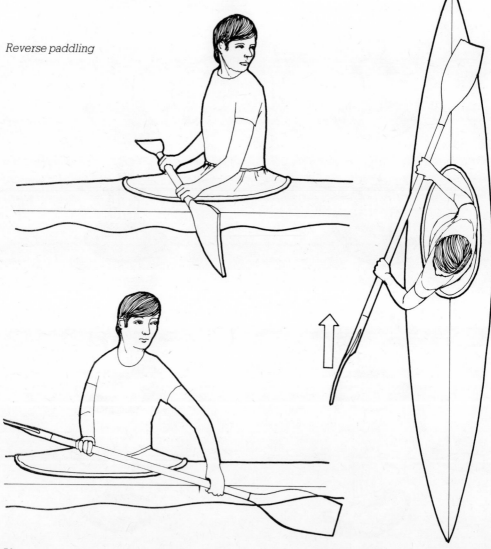

Reverse paddling

Stopping

Stop the canoe, when travelling forwards, by back paddling. Keep the paddle clear of the sides of the canoe, especially if you are moving fast, or the blade may go under the canoe and you will capsize.

Apply one stroke on either side of the canoe; if this does not stop you, apply another on each side until you do stop. If you apply an odd number of strokes the canoe will swing off course and you will lose directional control.

When you have tried this slowly, paddle forwards as fast as you can and stop as quickly as you can. Use an even number of strokes and try to keep the boat straight. This emergency stop is useful and should be practised.

To stop the canoe when travelling backwards, paddle forwards, again using an even number of strokes.

Stopping from forward travel

Turns

Because the curve along the side of the canoe is greater than that along the bottom, the turning circle of the canoe can be decreased by leaning the canoe on to its side throughout the turn. You must lean towards the supporting paddle and this is only possible while the paddle is moving through the water or the water is moving past the paddle. As the paddle stroke completes the turn, the legs must be used to bring the canoe upright again. (This does not apply to modern slalom kayaks.)

this curve is greater than

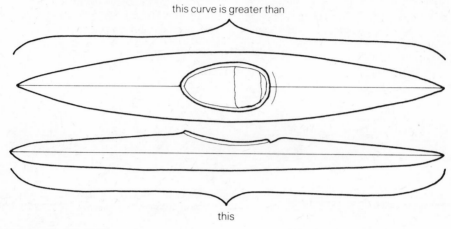

this

Forward sweep stroke

This is the simplest way of making a canoe turn and conversely of making a turning canoe go straight.

1   From a stationary position, turn from the waist so that you can reach well forward; put your paddle into the water close to the boat. Brace your knees and feet.
2   Sweep the paddle through the water with the whole blade submerged, so that it travels in a half circle as far away from the canoe as you can reach to the back of the canoe.

3   During this time, let the canoe lean over towards the paddle, holding it with your knees. This will increase your reach for added leverage and decrease the curve of the canoe in the water.
4   Before the paddle arrives at the end of the stroke – sit up by using your knees. You cannot lean on a stationary paddle.

(a) Lean well forward, with knees and feet braced, to begin turn

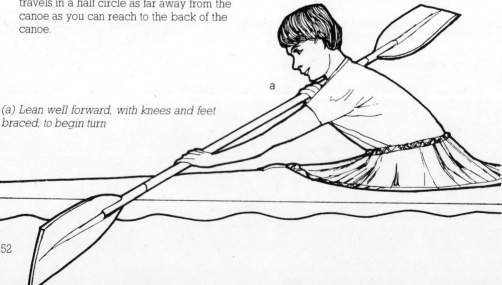

a

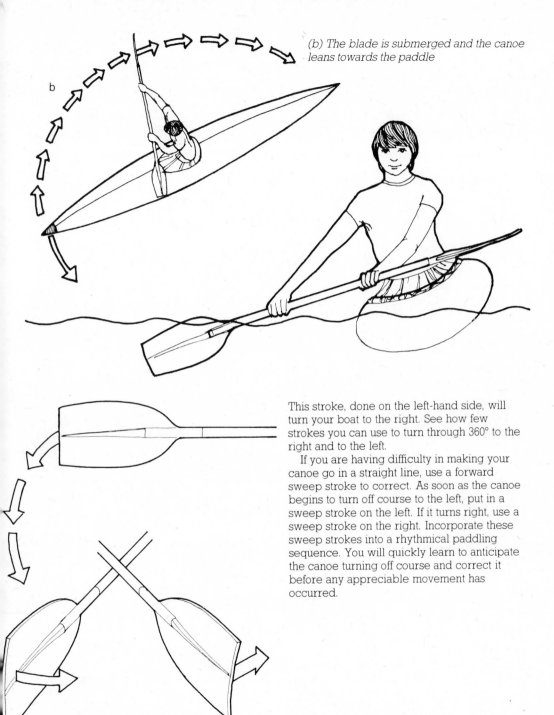

(b) The blade is submerged and the canoe leans towards the paddle

b

This stroke, done on the left-hand side, will turn your boat to the right. See how few strokes you can use to turn through 360° to the right and to the left.

If you are having difficulty in making your canoe go in a straight line, use a forward sweep stroke to correct. As soon as the canoe begins to turn off course to the left, put in a sweep stroke on the left. If it turns right, use a sweep stroke on the right. Incorporate these sweep strokes into a rhythmical paddling sequence. You will quickly learn to anticipate the canoe turning off course and correct it before any appreciable movement has occurred.

Paddle direction in sweep stroke

Reverse sweep stroke

A good, simple method of turning the boat.
Use the back of the blade.

1 Turn round and put the blade in the water
   behind you and close to the canoe. Do not
   alter your control hand or move either
   hand along the loom.
2 Sweep the blade forward through the
   water, pushing your hands out so that the
   paddle travels in a wide half circle to the
   front of the canoe.
3 Lean the canoe, using your legs, towards
   the paddle. Sit up again as the paddle
   reaches the front of the canoe.
4 The canoe turns towards the paddle.
5 Practise this stroke, on both sides,
   increasing the lean gradually.
6 Alternate a forward sweep on the right –
   you will be leaning right, with a reverse
   sweep on the left, leaning left. You must sit
   up and change the lean between strokes.
   You will turn your canoe easily through 360°
   and get used to leaning the canoe which is
   all important on moving water.

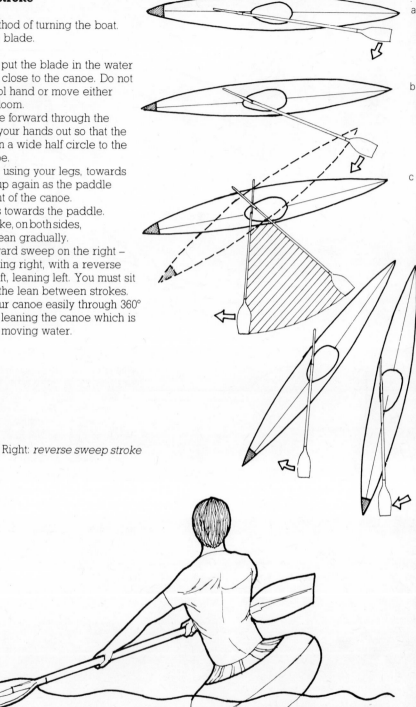

Right: *reverse sweep stroke*

The stroke in action

Low telemark turn

This is used for changing direction in fast moving water. To practise it in still water:

1 Paddle forwards at medium speed.
2 Finish the sequence with a forward sweep stroke on say, the left (a).
3 As the canoe starts to turn right, put the back of your right blade on the water well out from the side of the boat (b and c).
4 Lift the leading edge of the blade.
5 Press down on the paddle and away from the boat (d).

6 Lean on the paddle as the canoe turns (e).
7 Sit up as the turn is completed (f).

On moving water, you will be travelling along and need only provide the steering stroke and the lean.

A low telemark is also useful for turning alongside another canoe, the bank or a jetty. Practise it on both sides until you have the confidence to lean the canoe well over on to its side.

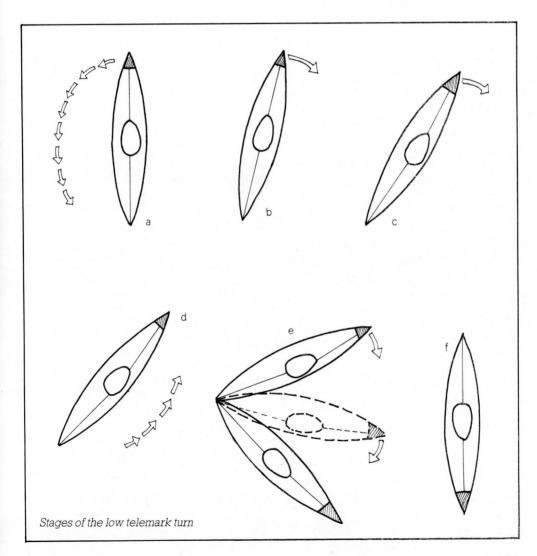

Stages of the low telemark turn

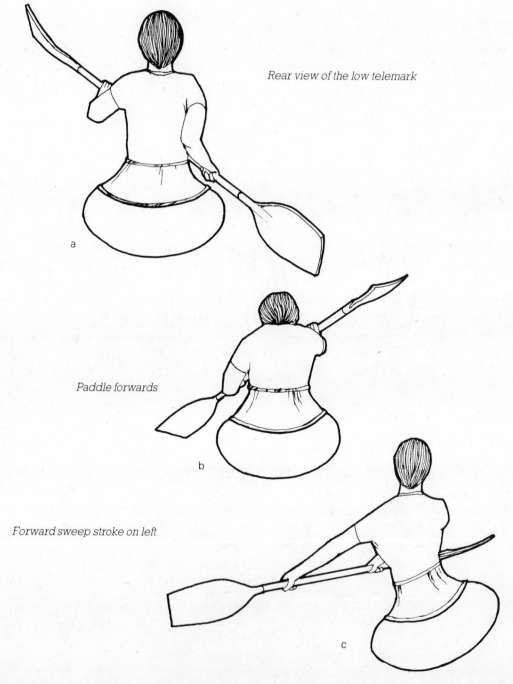

Rear view of the low telemark

a

Paddle forwards

b

Forward sweep stroke on left

c

Lifting leading edge. Low telemark on right

d

e

The completion of the turn

f

There are two support strokes you should learn at this stage.

'Slap' for support

This is oddly named as it is really a 'press' for support:

1 Hold your paddle in the usual way. Work on your control side first (a).

Working on the control side first

2 Without leaning the canoe, drop the paddle blade face (concave side) down, on to the water at right angles to and as far from the canoe as you can (b).

3 *On no account* slide your hands along the loom or allow your control hand to slip round the shaft. Instead, push your elbows forward so that the concave face is down on the water.

4 Press down briefly and sharply and feel the potential support (c).

5 Drop the hand so that the blade turns through 90° (d).

6 Lift the blade out of the water. Because the blade is vertical it will be easy to lift (d).

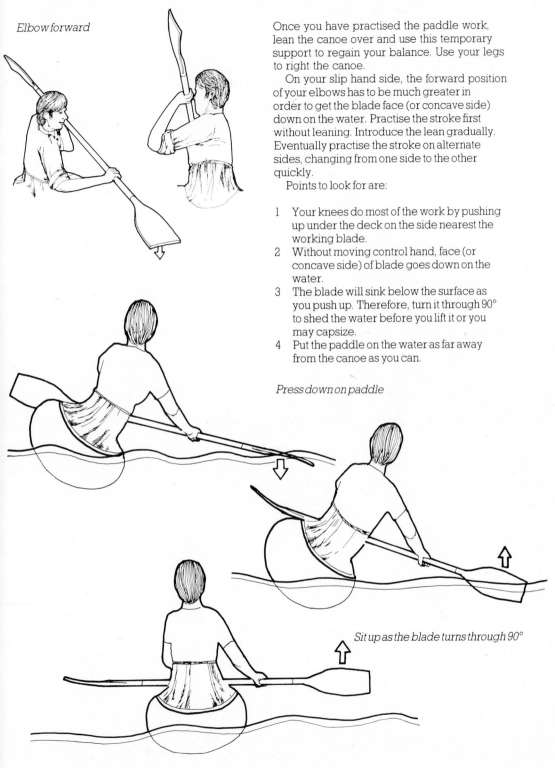

Elbow forward

Once you have practised the paddle work, lean the canoe over and use this temporary support to regain your balance. Use your legs to right the canoe.

On your slip hand side, the forward position of your elbows has to be much greater in order to get the blade face (or concave side) down on the water. Practise the stroke first without leaning. Introduce the lean gradually. Eventually practise the stroke on alternate sides, changing from one side to the other quickly.

Points to look for are:

1   Your knees do most of the work by pushing up under the deck on the side nearest the working blade.
2   Without moving control hand, face (or concave side) of blade goes down on the water.
3   The blade will sink below the surface as you push up. Therefore, turn it through 90° to shed the water before you lift it or you may capsize.
4   Put the paddle on the water as far away from the canoe as you can.

Press down on paddle

Sit up as the blade turns through 90°

Draw stroke

This moves the canoe sideways and also supports you. Practise without leaning the canoe:

1 Hold the paddle in the usual way (a).
2 Brace your legs.
3 Hold the paddle as near the vertical as you can.
4 Drop the bottom blade into the water at right angles to the boat and two feet/60 cm or more from it (b).

5 Lever the paddle into the vertical position by pushing the top hand across your body and using the lower hand as the fulcrum (c).
6 Before the blade touches the canoe (and capsizes you!) turn it through 90° until the concave face is towards the back of the canoe and lift it clear of the water (d).

The draw stroke

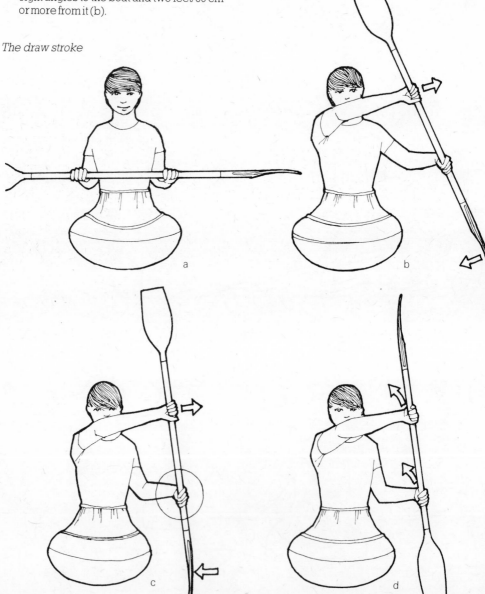

The draw stroke in action

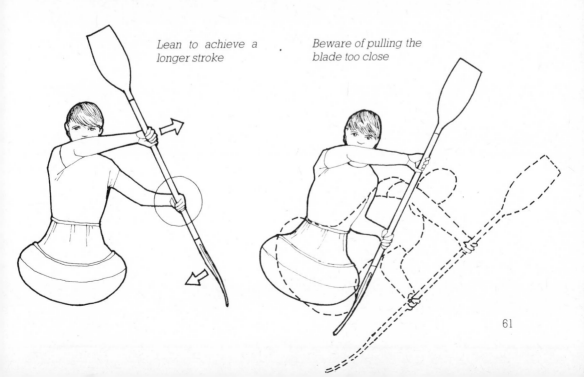

Lean to achieve a longer stroke

Beware of pulling the blade too close

7 You will have moved your canoe sideways by 6 to 8 ins./15 to 20 cm.
8 Experiment with leaning the canoe over so that you can make a longer stroke. Use your legs to sit up as you complete the stroke.
9 If you put the paddle into the water forward of where you are sitting the bow will be drawn round to the paddle.

If you put the paddle in behind you, the stern will be drawn round.

If you put the paddle in near the centre the whole canoe will move sideways.

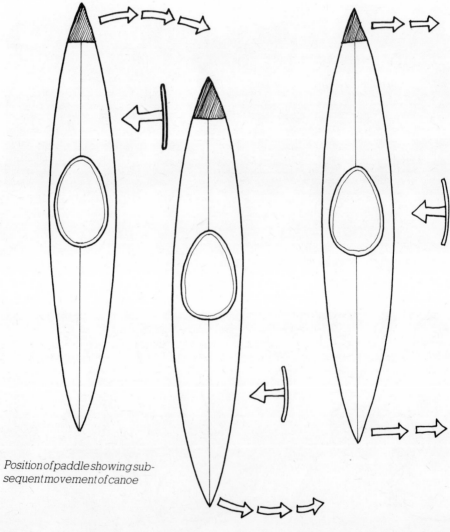

Position of paddle showing sub-sequent movement of canoe

Stern rudder

A useful steering stroke constantly used when travelling down wind and in surf:

1   The boat is moving forward, propelled by you, the wind or the wave.
2   To steer to the left, put the left blade in the water well behind you and very close to the canoe. Face of the blade towards the canoe.
3   Hold the paddle firmly in place.
4   Direction can be altered by pressing the back of the blade out against the moving water.

Using a stern rudder
(See also pages 117 and 118)

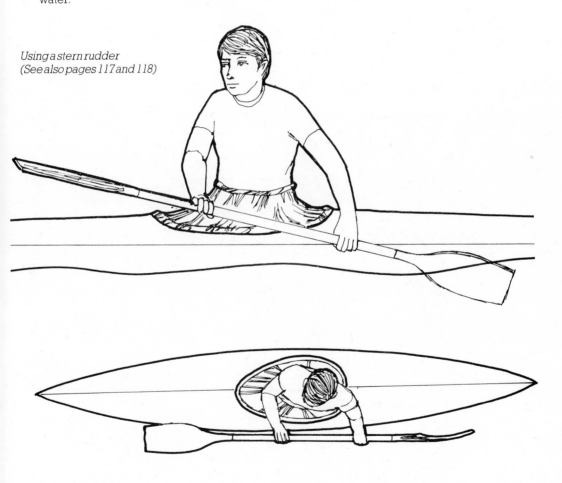

Capsize drill

Accept that sooner or later you will capsize accidentally. It is better to do so deliberately during one of your early sessions. You may even be lucky enough to practise in a swimming pool. Until you have capsized, wear your spraydeck, but do not fit it on to the canoe as you will have enough to think about the first time.

Check that the water is deep enough and free from obstructions, then:

1 Hold your paddle in the usual way.
2 Slowly roll over sideways into the water.
3 Sit quite still until the boat stops moving (a) and you are completely upside down. Now gravity will help you get out.

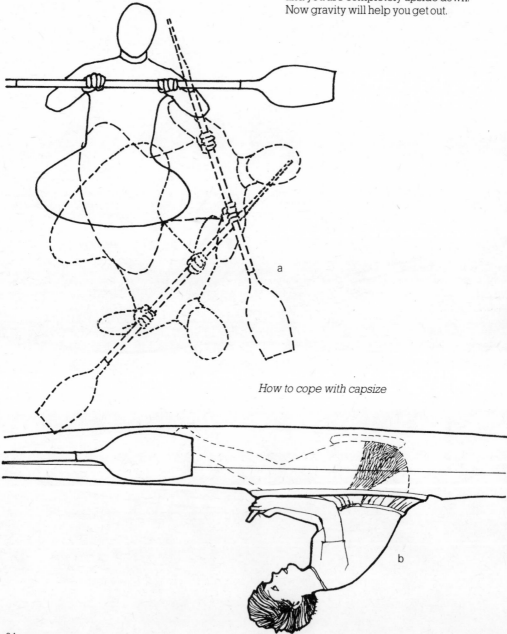

How to cope with capsize

Body movements after capsize

4 Let go of your paddle.
5 If wearing a spray deck, locate the release cord (open your eyes if you can). Pull firmly to release the elastic then run your fingers round the cockpit to remove the deck (b).
6 Put your hands on the sides of the canoe, behind you (c).
7 Keep your legs straight and quite still (d).
8 Lean forward as far as you can and slide carefully out of the canoe (e).
9 As you surface, gently put your hand on the canoe to stop it drifting or blowing away (f).

10 Leave the canoe upside down and undisturbed so that the cockpit remains under the water. The air trapped inside helps the canoe to float. (If you climb on to, tip or roll the canoe over, the air comes out and is replaced by more water making rescue more difficult.)

11 Go to one end of the canoe – maintain contact with the canoe all the time (g).

12 Locate the paddle. If necessary, tow the canoe to the paddle. *Never* let go of the canoe – even briefly. It will support you and is more easily seen than you alone.

13 Tow the canoe and paddle to the nearest shore. It is usually easiest to swim on your back. If the swim is a long one you may choose to inflate your lifejacket (h).

Try to move slowly and carefully all the time. Count from one to five in the upside-down position before pulling the release cord. Withdraw your straight legs slowly so that you do not bruise them on the cockpit rim. Practise the drill until you are as happy upside-down as the right way up.

Leave the canoe and tug it to the shore

66

Emptying the canoe

1 Float the canoe as close to the shore as you can.
2 The cockpit is down in the water and effectively sealed.
3 When you reach shallow water, break this seal by rolling the canoe on its side.
4 It is possible to damage a full canoe by lifting the two ends simultaneously without first breaking the seal.
5 With one person at each end, lift and lower alternate ends of the canoe until all the water is removed.
6 One person alone can usually empty the canoe by balancing the upturned canoe over the thighs.

Emptying a canoe

Emptying water from a capsized canoe

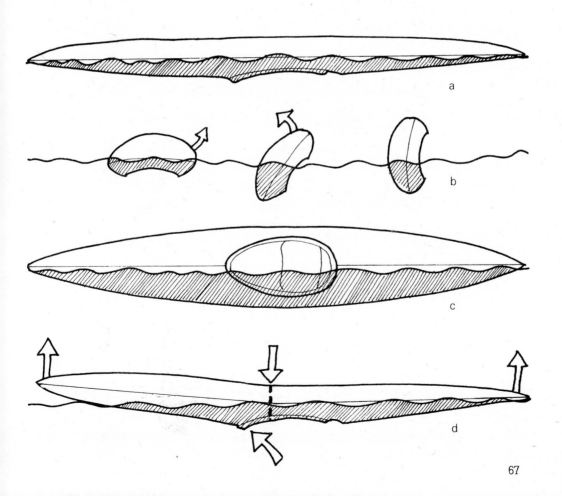

67

Deep-water rescue

Where it is not possible to go ashore to empty a capsized canoe, it is quick and easy to do so in the deep water. There are several methods but this is one of the best:

1 Patient waits quietly in the water holding the end of own canoe and paddle.
2 Rescuer approaches and gives bow of canoe to the patient. Patient remains on rescuer's bow throughout.
3 Rescuer takes both paddles and puts them in paddle park. See page 111.
4 Using two hands, rescuer takes patient's canoe, leaving it upside down throughout and floats it into a right angle with own canoe (b and c).
5 With a quick movement, rescuer lifts and pulls capsized canoe over his/her own deck until it will balance over own canoe (d).
6 Rescuer 'see-saws' capsized canoe until it is empty and then (e and f)
7 Rolls empty canoe right way up and drops it into the water, parallel to rescuing canoe with the back of it towards the patient (g).

Deep-water rescue

a

b

c

Lifting and emptying a capsized canoe

d

e

8 Rescuer lies across empty canoe (h).
9 Patient puts one hand on each canoe. Lies back in the water and swings his/her legs up into own cockpit (i).
10 Rescuer continues to lie across patient's canoe, holding canoes firmly together (j).
11 Patient pushes up into own canoe and puts on spraydeck (k).

Deep-water rescue

70

h

i

The rescuer keeps both canoes together

The patient returns to his own boat

j

k

12 If there is a lot of water in the canoe and
    the rescuer is unable to see-saw the boat
    as in 6, the patient can move along the
    deckline of the rescue canoe, take hold of
    his own deckline and lever down to assist
    the rescuer, then returning along the
    deckline to his original position. It is
    VITAL that actual physical contact is
    maintained between the patient and the
    canoes at all times as the different speeds
    or directions of wind and current can
    quickly separate the two.

This sort of cooper-
ation effects rescue
quickly and safely

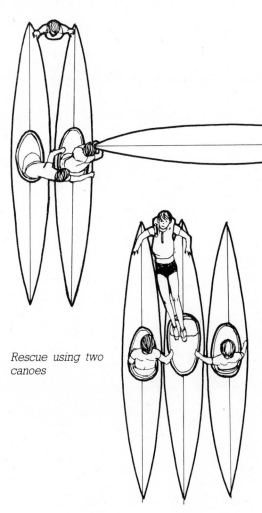

13　In very rough conditions, use two canoes to do the rescue, lying parallel and touching, the additional canoeist supporting the rescuer initially and subsequently assisting with emptying the capsized boat.

14　By forming a 'raft' of the three canoes, the patient is easily returned to his canoe. It is also useful, on exposed lakes or the sea, if group members not involved in the rescue, form a raft to minimize the risk of further capsizes. The raft can be used for resting or eating on a long trip.

These basic techniques will give you a good degree of control over your canoe and enable you to graduate to moving water.

Rescue using two canoes

The formation of a raft

Chapter Four
What Next?

The kayak is a versatile boat. It can be successfully paddled on most ponds, lakes, canals and rivers. It has crossed the Atlantic, the Tasman Sea and rounded Cape Horn. It is easily portable and relatively cheap. Canoeing can be enjoyed at any level from pottering about on a local pond, when a few simple skills will suffice, to National, International or Olympic standards requiring the highest degree of fitness and technical ability. It has no age limits; it is enjoyed by young and old alike and many disabled people find they can join canoe clubs on equal terms with the able-bodied.

How do you find out what sort of canoeing suits you?

Undoubtedly the easiest way is to join a local canoe club. Most clubs have a bias towards a particular branch of canoeing but will also offer opportunities for trying a variety of boats and water. Many instructional courses will do the same. The following is a list of the possibilities. Most of the canoeing described can be pursued at levels from light-hearted entertainment to dedicated involvement.

Canoeing for leisure

A large number of people enjoy canoeing at a very uncomplicated level, choosing to canoe on calm inland water in good weather. Pottering is an excellent way of enjoying the countryside and is thoroughly recommended. Almost any general-purpose canoe would be suitable provided it is sound and has adequate buoyancy. Most people have a suitable piece of water close to home, but it would still be worth joining the local canoe club for additional facilities. Wear your lifejacket and seek permission before going afloat.

Wild water race on the River Dee (William G. Sampson)

Canoe touring and camping: sea and inland

A logical progression from pottering and a relaxation from competitive canoeing, touring is the ideal way of spending a day, or longer, on the water. Touring canoes can be for one or two people which makes them especially suitable for group or family use. Touring or general-purpose canoes are usually relatively wide with little rocker and capable of carrying camping equipment. It is perfectly possible to use slalom canoes for touring, possibly adding a skeg (see page 109) and carrying minimum equipment.

There are many preparations to be made before embarking on a tour. The following headings should help you plan your trip:

Select the area: a river; lakes and river; river and estuary to the sea; sea.

Map and books: buy relevant maps and guides (approach your National Canoe Association first).

Weather: check the general weather patterns in your chosen area.

Access: obtain permission to launch, land and camp at suitable places.

Group: choose a route technically suited to the group and its equipment.

Canoes must be suitable for the type of water; in good repair; capable of carrying equipment; contain sufficient buoyancy.

Transport: work out any problems. Consider use of non-canoeing drivers.

Personal clothing: adequate but not bulky.

Food and fuel: adequate supplies must be carried or bought. Check availability.

Drinking water: no problem on inland waters, but needs careful planning on sea trips.

Hygiene: unless using organized campsites large groups of canoeists may have to carry a latrine tent and digging tool. Small groups should at least carry a trowel in order to avoid any risk to health.

Tents: of necessity, these must be small and lightweight.

Stoves: choose one for which fuel is portable and readily available.

Sleeping bags: any good-quality bag, depending on how much you can afford. Man-made fibre dries out more quickly than down!

Miscellaneous: canoe touring is an ideal opportunity for photography, bird-watching, sketching etc., so take the necessary items.

Single touring canoe (429×61cm)

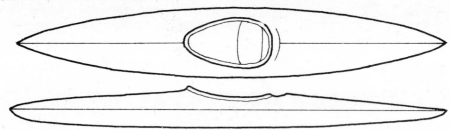

Double touring canoe (483×79cm)

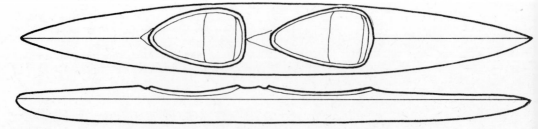

Canoe tour on the Dee

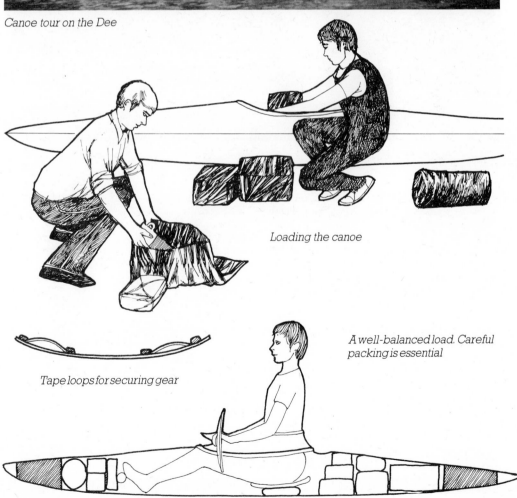

Loading the canoe

Tape loops for securing gear

A well-balanced load. Careful packing is essential

Canoe campsite

Escort boats: there has, in the past, been some pressure brought to bear on canoeists to use some form of escort vessel on open water trips. Generally speaking, escort boats have not proved satisfactory as they lack the versatility of the kayaks. In the hands of a competent helmsman an escort boat could be valuable on some trips but would do nothing for the peace, quiet and independence enjoyed by canoeists.

Canoe-camping is a way of life. It is impossible to do it justice in these notes. If you have not done any camping, practise in the garden, or close to home before setting off. All the gear must be packed in waterproof bags (page 24) which must be small enough to slide into the canoe. The bags should be secured by wedging tightly or by tying them in to tape loops fibreglassed to the canoe. Meticulous care is needed when canoe-camping to keep all equipment dry, particularly your sleeping bag, one set of clothes, a towel and some matches or a lighter.

Finally, load the canoe on the principle of things needed last go in first and spread the weight from end to end and from side to side, so that the canoe will float level. Load the canoe in or very close to the water; it could be damaged by carrying when loaded. Keep the area where you sit completely free from gear.

Surfing

Many canoeists enjoy surfing as part of their sea-canoeing activities and spend time riding waves on a beach. It is often included in a sea-canoeing week-end with a day of surfing and a coastal tour. The weather conditions dictate the actual programme.

Surfing is also a competitive sport. Competitions are held at different venues and there are events for men and women in both slalom and surf kayaks. In a variety of events points are awarded for technical performances carried out in a given time.

Slalom at Shepperton Weir (William G. Sampson)

Canoeing as a sport

Serious canoe competition is only for the young and fit, prepared to accept regular coaching and train hard. However, it is possible to enjoy an occasional marathon race or novice slalom without being totally committed, although some training would be advisable.

Slalom

A slalom course consists of about half a mile of wild-water river, over which are hung anything from fifteen to thirty gates. Each gate consists of two poles. The race is against the clock and the canoeist must negotiate the numbered gates in the correct order. Gates are specifically forward or reverse, up or downstream and are marked accordingly. The red and white pole are on the canoeist's left as he goes through the gate and the green and white on his right. Any infringement and penalty time faults are added to the number of seconds taken to complete the course. Each

competitor has two runs, the fastest of which is counted. The gates are carefully positioned by the course designer to test technique and the ability to read the water. Competition is fierce and competitors work through a series of divisions to the top. It is a world championship event but an exhilarating experience at whatever level you compete.

Wild-water racing

Often run in conjunction with a slalom event but over a longer section of the river. The race is against the clock, taking the fastest line downstream. There are no gates or introduced hazards. The canoes are designed to travel fast in straight lines. It is a world championship event.

Sprint racing

Sprint racing is an Olympic event and is staged over distances of 500, 1000 and 10,000 metres. The kayak classes are for K-class boats and the number following the K indicates the number of crew, there being K1,

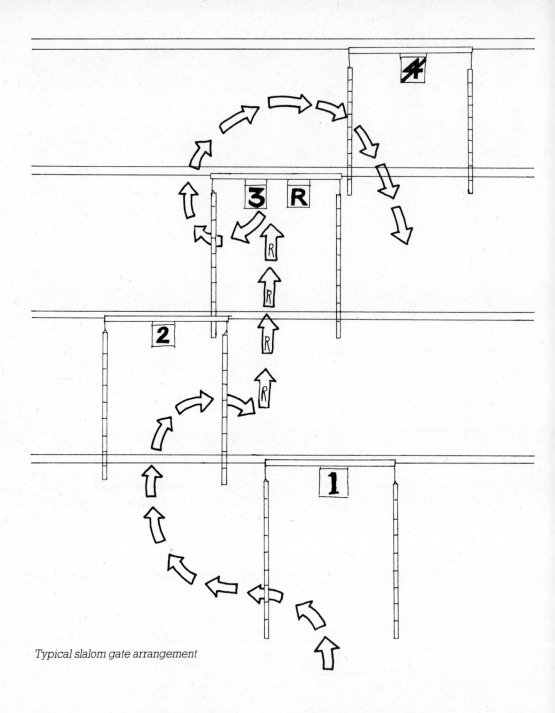

Typical slalom gate arrangement

Right: *The British Open Slalom Championships*

K2 and K4. Races are run under regatta conditions on still water. It is a sport for the dedicated paddler and the enthusiast is recommended to join a club specializing in sprint-canoeing.

Espada K1

To encourage young racers, the Espada Youth Kayak has been developed in Britain. Canoes or moulds are available to *bona-fide* groups wishing to promote Sprint Racing for young people. For further information write to The Espada Youth Scheme, c/o British Canoe Union.

Opposite: *Ladies slalom, Kayak class* (Chris Hawkesworth)

Opposite below: *Wild water race, River Dee* (Chris Hawkesworth)

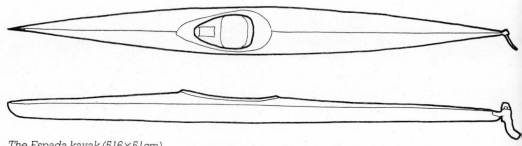

The Espada kayak (516×51cm)

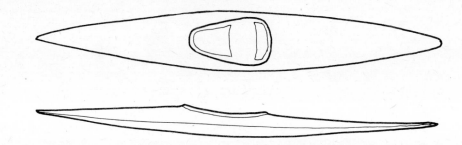

The modern slalom canoe (401×60cm)

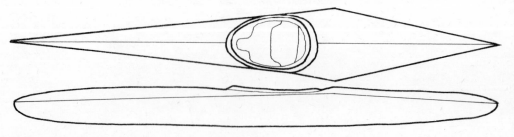

Wild water racing kayak (450×61cm)

Marathon

Once unique to Britain, this is now an international event. Staged over distances from five miles upwards, paddlers most frequently use specially designed K1 and K2 class kayaks. One common feature of the marathon race is the 'portage', where the crew must carry the boat round an obstacle (unshootable weir, lock, etc.) before paddling on. Races are held at a variety of venues on canals, rivers, estuaries and the sea. Competition is strong and individuals and team members compete for an overall points victory.

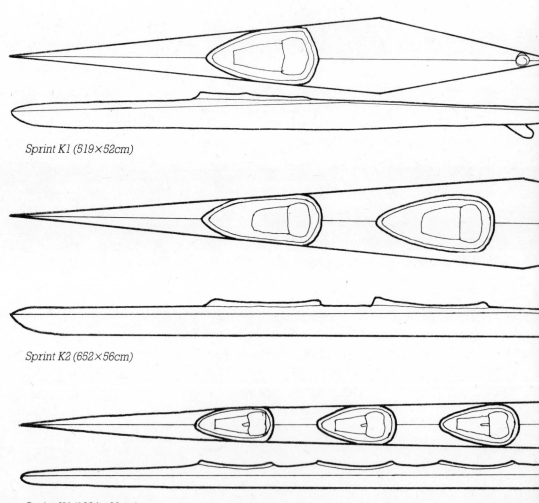

Sprint K1 (519×52cm)

Sprint K2 (652×56cm)

Sprint K4 (1094×60cm)

Wild water race (Chris Hawkesworth)

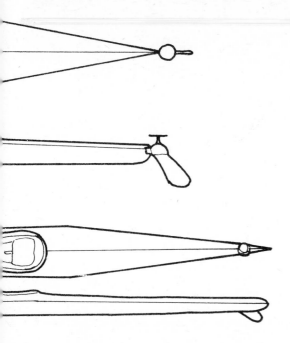

Above: *Canoe polo*

Left: *Bat canoe for polo (219×59cm)*

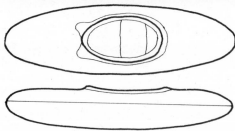

Canoe polo

An exciting game originally designed for stimulating interest in swimming-pool canoeing. It now stands as a branch of canoeing in its own right and is an international event.

Canoe-sailing

It is possible to adapt a double touring canoe to a sailing canoe with the addition of mast, sails, lee boards and rudder. This is a great compromise and not particularly successful.

International 10 square metre canoe

The thoroughbred of canoe-sailing, this canoe is a sophisticated single-handed boat more identifiable with a sailing dinghy than a canoe. It is an international class with a small but dedicated following.

Teaching

As an experienced canoeist, you may eventually find you would like to introduce others to canoeing. Many canoe associations, schools and clubs run schemes with which you could get involved. In the first instance contact your local canoe club. The British Canoe Union organizes a set of personal proficiency tests which can lead on to Instructor qualifications.

Corps of Canoe Lifeguards

The corps began in 1960. It aims to train young people to a high degree of canoeing and rescue skills so that they are able to offer assistance in times of flood or accident on river or sea. They are also available to teach other young people to canoe. Their skills are recognized and called upon by coastguard, police and local authorities. Further information from the Secretary, CCLG, c/o British Canoe Union.

The insignia and rescue canoe of the Canoe Lifeguards

Many people find they get maximum satisfaction from canoeing by combining several aspects. It is worth trying out a variety of boats and water before concentrating on one particular event.

10 square metre canoe

Chapter Five
River Canoeing

Water flowing downstream in a natural river will always behave in a particular way. It is predictable. This means that you can learn to understand, or read, the movements of the water and paddle your canoe accordingly. It is not the strongest person who is most successful in river canoeing but the one who reads the water most accurately.

Behaviour of water

Water running downstream in a straight section of river with no obstacles, will move faster in the middle than at the sides, where friction against the bank will slow it down. In a fast flowing river this can mean that the water near the bank will flow upstream and there will be a distinct line between the two directions of water. It therefore follows that if you want to travel downstream you should paddle down the middle of the river and if you want to travel upstream you should paddle very close to the bank.

As soon as the river bends, the main stream will follow the outside of that bend. Here the water will accelerate, run deeply and probably undercut the bank. Where the bank is tree-lined there will be branches overhanging the water and some trees may have fallen into the river. On the inside of the bend, the water will be slow moving and shallow from the silting up process. It is usually the outside of the bend that gives the best route downstream as long as the trees are avoided.

Any obstacle in the river will alter the direction of the flow of the water. If the bank projects into the current, the water will accelerate round the piece of bank and on the downstream side of the projection the water

Wild water in the River Teme
(William G. Sampson)

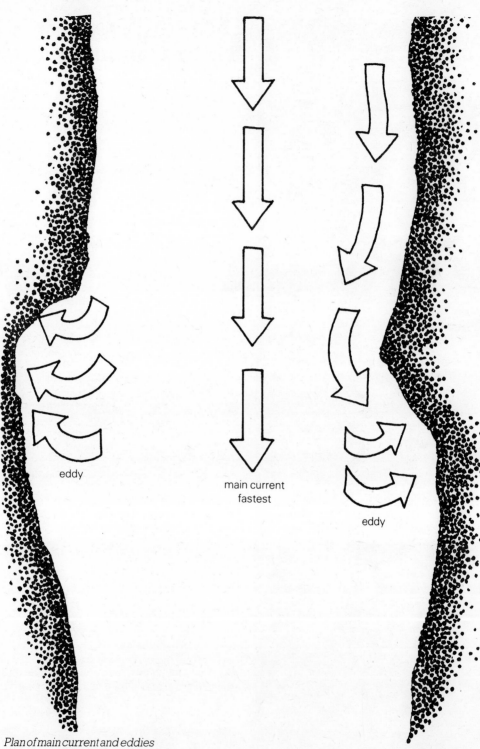

eddy

main current
fastest

eddy

Plan of main current and eddies

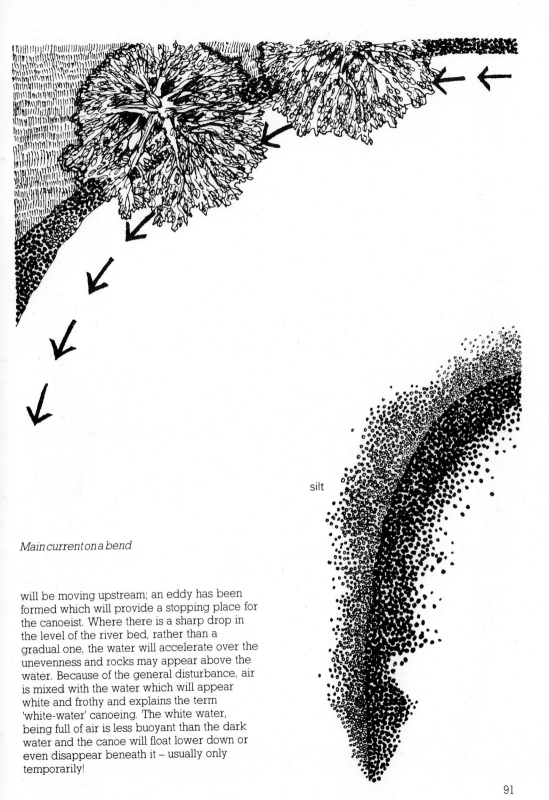

silt

Main current on a bend

will be moving upstream; an eddy has been formed which will provide a stopping place for the canoeist. Where there is a sharp drop in the level of the river bed, rather than a gradual one, the water will accelerate over the unevenness and rocks may appear above the water. Because of the general disturbance, air is mixed with the water which will appear white and frothy and explains the term 'white-water' canoeing. The white water, being full of air is less buoyant than the dark water and the canoe will float lower down or even disappear beneath it – usually only temporarily!

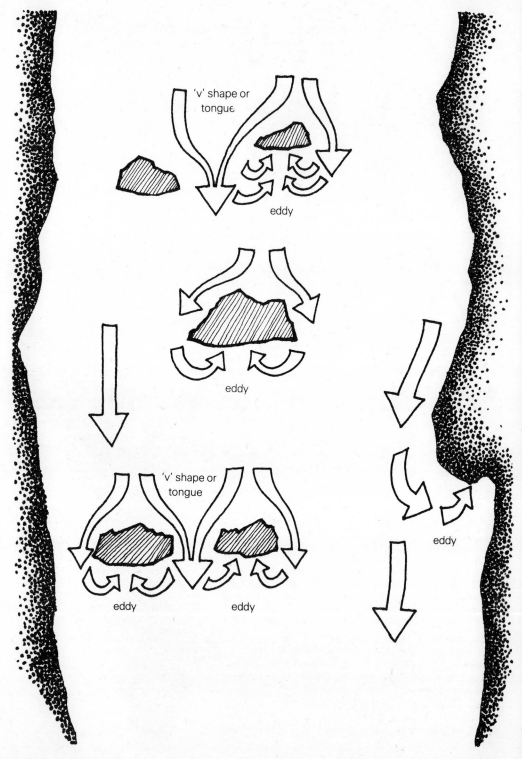

All the rocks on the river bed will divert the flow of water as does the shape of the bank. Irregularities of the bank, and rocks which are above the water will cause horizontal movement and submerged rocks and irregularities in the river bed will cause horizontal and vertical movement. Downstream of exposed rocks and those only just submerged will be an area of calm water, an eddy, which will be stationary in a slow moving river and travelling upstream in a faster one. Where there is a series of rocks spread through one of those rapid sections of river, the overall appearance will be confused. Do not let this confuse you! Look at each rock and identify the main current and the eddy. Submerged rocks may only give themselves away by the eddy they create and those only just submerged by a hump in the water level followed by an eddy. Two rocks close to each other will push the water into a V-shape or tongue, with the mouth of the V upstream. You will need time as you approach a rapid to pick out the biggest tongue, which is likely to give the main route downstream, and then to line up your canoe. You will also have to re-align your canoe for the next tongue, and the next. It is always useful to get out of your canoe above a rapid and look at the problems from the bank. Where the water drops over a ledge, natural or artificial, the falling water will go below the level of the water and re-surface in a circular movement so that the top layer is travelling upstream and will be white and frothy. This water pattern is called a 'stopper', as in heavy water the canoeist paddling over the fall will have to paddle hard to avoid being stopped short by the reverse flow.

This then is the basic information you need to understand the water and take advantage of the bits which are going the way you want to go. Take every opportunity to observe water behaviour, even in small streams, and you will soon be capable of reading your way down a rapid.

Left: *Tongues and eddies produced by rocks*

Below: *A 'stopper'*

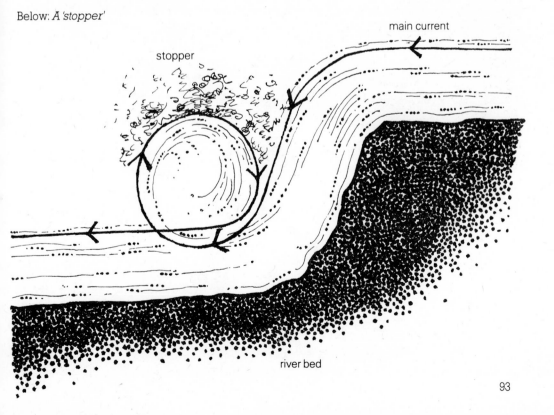

main current

stopper

river bed

Further techniques

All the basic techniques you have already learnt are useful on moving water. There are also a few extra manoeuvres to be learnt. Choose a medium pace river with plenty of space between rapids. If possible go with a competent canoeist who knows the river. To avoid unnecessary frustration remember that the water in the river will be flowing up and downstream.

Launching

Launch your canoe with the bow upstream. The current will help hold the boat into the bank. In a strong eddy launch bow downstream for the same reason.

The most effective way to turn your canoe is to paddle the front half of it out into the current and let that current carry the bow round and downstream. Then paddle the front half back into the slack water at the side and let the

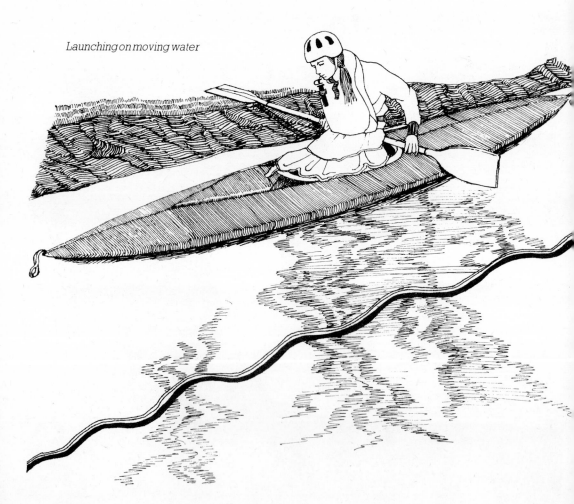

Launching on moving water

current carry the back half downstream. You could continue to turn your canoe this way round for a long time as the water is doing the work. It is now vital that you lean the canoe to assist the turn. You must always present the hull of the canoe to the current, which means if you are turning right, lean to the right; if you are turning left lean to the left. If you lean upstream, the water will catch the deck of the canoe and you will capsize immediately. It is especially important to lean as you turn into the current and even more important to change the lean as you turn back out of it.

Break in

From any stopping place, by the bank or behind a rock, facing upstream, you will need to turn into the current to continue down river. Let the water turn you. Paddle hard forwards across the dividing line between the eddy and main current. Aim to get the front third of your canoe over that line. As the current swings your bow downstream, use a low telemark and plenty of lean on the downstream side. Sit up as soon as you can and paddle away down river. As you gain confidence you may prefer to use a high telemark or draw stroke in place of the low telemark. (See illustrations A, B and C).

Use of current to break in

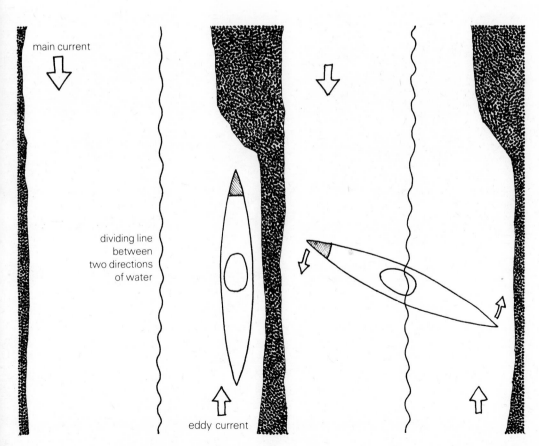

main current

dividing line
between
two directions
of water

eddy current

Completing break in

96

Break out

Travelling downriver you must be able to stop at the bank or in an eddy. Line your canoe up so that you are heading straight down river towards and slightly to one side of your chosen stopping place. Just before you reach it, use a forward sweep stroke to drive the front third of the canoe into the eddy – more than one stroke may be needed – do not give up too soon. As the bow enters the eddy it will swing upstream. The main current will continue to carry the stern down river – lean into the turn and use a reverse sweep stroke or low telemark to support you and complete the turn. You will be facing upstream neatly tucked in

to the eddy. As with breaking in you will soon prefer to use the high telemark instead of the low telemark. It is well worth practising breaking in and breaking out at every opportunity until you have the confidence to use them on the rapid sections of the river.

*Break out behind a
rock*

Ferry glide – forward

A manoeuvre which enables you to cross a current without drifting downstream. By holding the canoe at an angle, the water against the hull pushes the canoe across the river. Choose an obstacle-free area for practice. From slack water at the edge point the bow of the canoe upstream and into the current. Hold the canoe firmly with your legs and lean downstream. Keep the angle acute or the bow will be turned downstream. (If this happens turn it into a break in and start all over again). Now keep paddling forwards on both sides. Keep the bow almost directly into the current to start with. If you find you are travelling upstream, let the bow swing downstream a little as the object is to cross the current from one side to the other. As the current will vary in speed across the river so will you have to constantly adjust the angle of the canoe. The faster the water, the more acute the angle. Use forward paddling strokes on one or both sides. Avoid using a reverse stroke as it is unbalancing and less effective. Remember it is easy to allow the bow to swing downstream a little and difficult, if not impossible, to drive it back upstream from a position sideways on to the the current. As you enter the slack water or eddy on the far side, change the lean. If you get the angle right, anything from 15° to 45°, the water will take you across with minimum of effort. It is well worth practising until you can feel the correct angle every time.

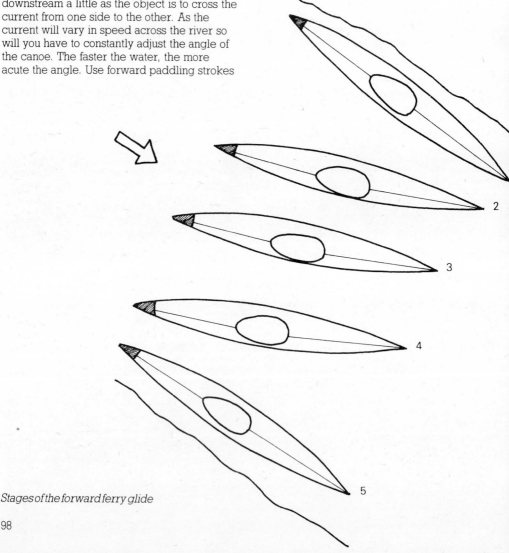

Stages of the forward ferry glide

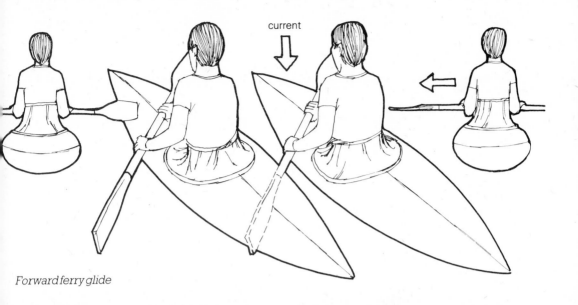

current

Forward ferry glide

On the River Nidd

Ferry glide – reverse

The same manoeuvre carried out facing downstream. More difficult as you cannot see the variations in water speed so easily. Also more valuable as it can be used to hold your position on the river and give you time to avoid obstacles. From your position of paddling down river, stop your canoe by back paddling. Swing the stern slightly to left or right, towards which ever bank you want to move. Keep the angle very acute until you are sure you can maintain the angle. Lean downstream and continue to back paddle to maintain the angle. Look over your downstream shoulder at the variations in water speed and to check on whether or not you are gaining or losing ground in relation to the bank.

Reverse ferry glide

current

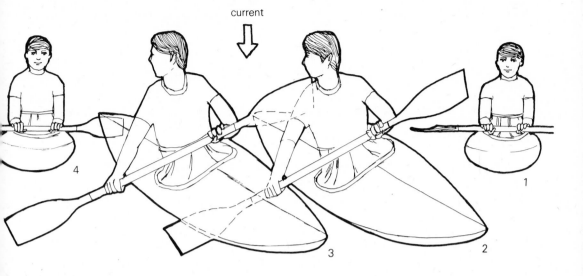

4　　　　　　　3　　　　　　　2　　　　　　　1

Reverse ferry glide

Lean upstream, like this, and you may capsize

High cross

This involves crossing a large tongue of water just below the point where it drops over a ledge. It works on the ferry-glide principle of paddling to hold the canoe at an angle while the water pushes you across. There will probably be a stopper formation to negotiate which makes for an exhilarating ride. From your position in slack water high up by the ledge, paddle hard into the current as if you were trying to paddle up the tongue of water. Be ready to lean downstream. Paddle until the front of your canoe is beyond the stopper and is in the slot, or dip, on the upstream side. You are sitting on the top of the stopper. The stopper may hold you there – just paddle gently for balance – be ready to lean downstream if the canoe turns. Now allow the bow to turn downstream a fraction, support yourself with a low or high telemark or draw stroke, lean downstream and you will fly across the tongue. Turn upstream into the eddy on the other side and lean hard into that turn.

Negotiating obstacles

To control your canoe on moving water you must be moving faster or slower than the water. If you travel at the same speed you will not be able to steer. You must therefore always be using your paddle either forwards or backwards. Your first rapid will announce itself by noise and then the river will drop away below you. Immediately swing the stern of your canoe towards the bank and reverse ferry glide. Get out on to the bank and have a good look at the rapid. You will get a lot of information by looking back up the rapid from lower down. Pick out the best route and serious obstacles such as fallen trees. Back in the canoe, reverse ferry glide to your chosen starting point, straighten up your canoe, paddle hard into the tongue and enjoy yourself. Always keep the canoe straight by vigorous paddling. If you do get turned round, paddle on backwards. At all costs, avoid floating down sideways or you will inevitably get stuck across a rock. If this does happen, immediately lean downstream on to the rock,

High cross

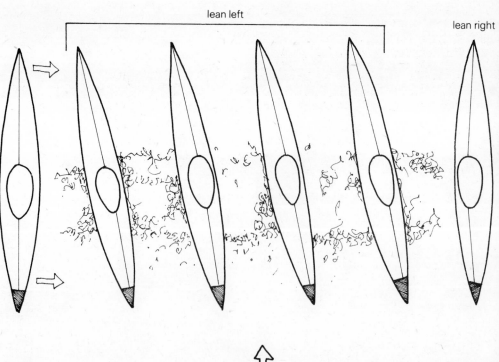

lean left

lean right

current

presenting the hull to the current. Use your hands, paddle or both and all your strength to lever the canoe round the rock. If for a second you lean upstream you will capsize and the boat will be badly damaged.

If you are heading for a rock or tree you must do one of two things:

1 Make a very early move to paddle forwards across the river. This is hazardous as it is easy to underestimate the speed at which you are moving and to be carried on to the obstacle sideways on.
2 Reverse ferry glide across the river until you can avoid the obstacle. This is the better choice as it slows you down as well as giving you more control. If you are uncertain of your reverse ferry glide, turn round quickly and use a forward one.

Never be tempted to get hold of an overhanging tree. Duck underneath branches but do not hold on – you will capsize and may get tangled up in the tree.

If at all possible make several descents of the same rapid. Paddle straight through once or twice. Then paddle down backwards. Now try ferry gliding across the rapid and taking various routes. Break out behind as many rocks as you can. Paddle back up the rapid by moving up in the eddies and ferry gliding from one eddy to another. If the water is too strong to get right back up the rapid, you will have to carry the canoe back to the top.

Capsize in moving water

As soon as you capsize you and your canoe will travel at the same speed as the water. Hold on to your canoe and if possible, your paddle. If the canoe is jammed, use all your strength to free it quickly and try to prevent the water getting in by keeping the cockpit facing downstream. Once the canoe is floating hold on to the upstream end, keep it away from your face, and steer the canoe straight down the rapid. You may have to use your feet on the rocks to help. If you are sure you can get to the bank without getting your canoe sideways on to the current, do so. If in any doubt, concentrate on keeping the canoe straight and clear of rocks and float down into the slack water at the bottom of the rapid – and smile!

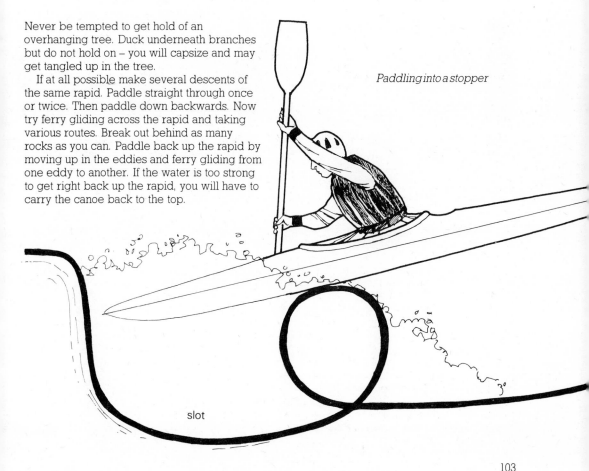

Paddling into a stopper

slot

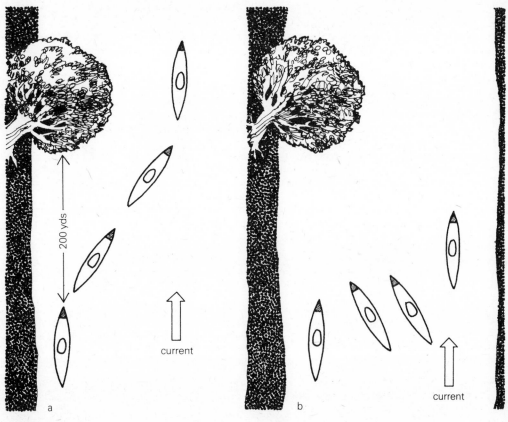

200 yds

current

a

current

b

Negotiating obstacles. Reverse ferry glide (b) to avoid obstacle

Right: *Negotiating Richmond Falls* (William G. Sampson)

Spate rivers

In many countries some of the best wild-water canoeing takes place when rivers are in spate, either from heavy rain, melting snow or the controlled release of stored water. However, a river in spate has additional hazards. Many extra trees will be included in the river, some growing, some fallen in and partly submerged. It is both unpleasant and dangerous to be strained out of your canoe by one of these. There may be large amounts of timber and rubbish floating in the river. Wire and other types of fences may be hidden from view. Stoppers may be huge and impossible to get out of. Bridges may suddenly appear at eye level. The general difficulty of the river will be greater and the water may be much colder. Unless you are with experts, keep away from spate rivers.

Weirs

Man-made weirs are best avoided until you are more experienced at reading water or are able to canoe with more experienced people. Unlike natural obstacles, weirs, locks and sluice gates may have contours below the water line which cause the water to behave unnaturally and it is possible for the inexperienced canoeist to become trapped. There is also a possibility that the remains of old structures may be lying in the water to add to the dangers. Bridge pillars can be treated as rocks unless they are of an open metal construction, in which case, keep well clear. Hydro-electric schemes too should be avoided as in some designs the intake area could be dangerous.

River capsize technique. Stay on the upstream end (a) and to one side (b)

Additional gear

In addition to your usual canoeing clothing, lifejacket or buoyancy aid and well fitting spray deck, you will need for a day out on a wild-water river: crash helmet, food, hot drink, change of clothing, towel, simple first aid kit (insect repellent, elastoplast, etc.) roll of adhesive canoe tape.

Within the group you should also carry spare paddles, and a 500 gauge 6 by 4 foot polythene bag for emergency shelter. All of these need to be in waterproof bags or bottles. Your canoe should have some extra buoyancy and toggles on bow and stern.

Transport

For a one-way river trip at least two vehicles will be needed. If it is a group outing one larger vehicle and trailer with one additional car is ideal. The two vehicles go to the starting place and people, canoes and gear are dropped off. The two vehicles and trailer then go to the finish, the large vehicle and trailer are left and the two drivers return to the start in the car. If you are a smaller group, canoes can be carried on roof racks and the same procedure followed. You may even be lucky and find a non-canoeist willing to do the driving, which saves a lot of time.

Gradings or difficulty ratings

Many wild-water rivers are graded on a rating system table from 1, very easy, to 6, extremely difficult (see page 168).

Gradings are based on speed of current, gradient of falls, width of stream, portages, diversion dams or low-water areas. They are also proportional to water temperature. As the temperature drops below 50°F., the difficulty rating goes up at least one grade. Spate conditions may raise or lower the gradings.

Few rivers have a single grading throughout. Most will have a general grade with specific sections being individually graded.

Do check water levels and temperatures and get the relevant information on gradings from the Canoe Association of the country where you will be canoeing. Be honest in the assessment of your own skills and do not attempt a higher grade unless you are with more experienced canoeists.

Legal aspects

The legal situation with regard to access and usage of canoeable inland waters is complex. In Britain, apart from a few rivers which have ancient public navigation rights, all water is private and permission must be obtained from riparian owners and all other interested parties. In the United States of America Federal and State legislation may apply. Intending paddlers should check with the Attorney General of the State concerned and with the local Fish and Game Department. In most other countries, there are fewer restrictions but it is always safer to check with the National Canoe Association of the country concerned.

In all cases, membership of a recognized canoe club will give you access to the relevant information and will also assist you and others to obtain access to rivers.

Chapter Six
Sea-Canoeing

The sea may appear an awesome place to go canoeing, and sea-canoeing is not to be undertaken without some thought and preparation. However, there are many ordinary canoeists who safely take their kayaks on the sea and numbers are increasing rapidly. The sea offers all the excitement and interest you could wish for plus freedom of movement and exploration not so easily found in other branches of canoeing.

In addition to basic canoeing techniques already learnt, you will need to be able to handle your canoe in waves and effect rescues in off shore situations. You will need a suitable canoe and some additional equipment. Finally, a working knowledge of maps, charts, tidal streams, weather interpretation and navigation are all necessary. If the list is formidable, remember that you will learn the skills over a period of time, especially if you are able to accompany other sea canoeists.

Suitable canoes

Most touring and slalom canoes can be easily adapted for sea-canoeing without making permanent alterations. The following adaptations are recommended.

Fixed rudder or skeg.

To increase the directional stability of some touring canoes and all slalom canoes. This removable fibreglass skeg gives the canoe longer waterline length and makes it easier to steer in straight lines. It slides on over the stern, is fixed on with elastic cord and easily released for coming ashore. It can be bought from some canoe manufacturers or made at home.

Surfing in on a big wave

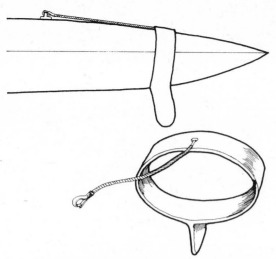

Detachable fibreglass skeg for improved directional stability

Paddling close inshore

Additional buoyancy

To facilitate deep-water rescues, extra buoyancy is important. Fill any available space, excluding the cockpit area, with air bags, polystyrene blocks or waterproof bags of gear.

Deck fittings

In addition to the usual bow and stern loops or toggles, deck lines are essential for maintaining contact with a capsized canoe and for quick rescues. The layout must suit the individual but any system should keep the cockpit clear of entangling lines.

Spare paddles, maps, compass and flares can be held by elastic cord.

The paddle park, which keeps the paddle floating alongside the canoe while you eat, check the map or rescue another canoe, is also elastic.

A towing line can be useful and should be located centrally behind the cockpit or well forward on one side of the cockpit. It should be easily released from rescuer or patient.

All these fittings should be placed to give minimum interference with normal paddling.

Deck strength.

Some lightweight kayaks may need the deck strengthening in front of the cockpit in order to stand up to the additional strain of deep-water rescues.

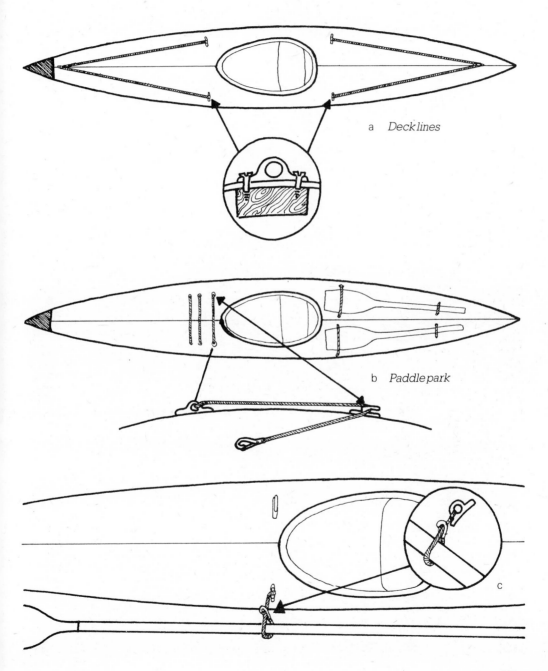

a   *Deck lines*

b   *Paddle park*

c

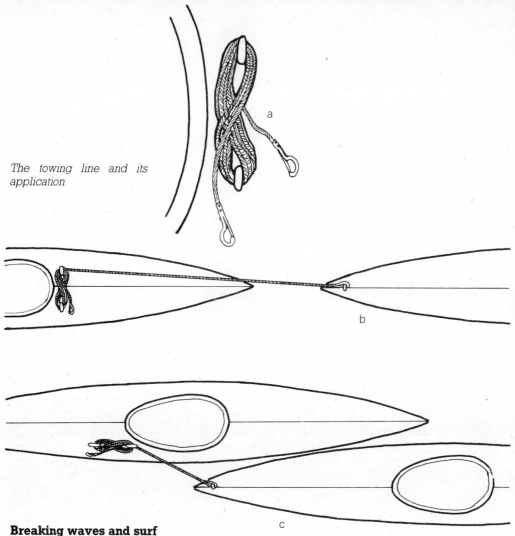

The towing line and its application

a

b

c

Breaking waves and surf

Handling your canoe in breaking sea waves is an exciting experience. Many people concentrate on this aspect of canoeing and it can be a highly technical and competitive area. The basic techniques given here are aimed at getting you safely on to and off a beach through breaking waves and coping with the waves you will meet on a coastal canoe trip. They will also give you an introduction to canoe-surfing in its own right.

Find a sandy beach with small waves, less than three feet high, breaking on to it. Choose an area away from rocks and tide rips (see page 128) and clear of other canoeists, board surfers and bathers. If the wind is blowing strongly out to sea, wait for another day.

Sea kayak

If you decide to concentrate on sea-canoeing, there are several excellent sea kayaks on the market. The designs are taken directly from original Eskimo kayaks and they are well suited to sea conditions. Many have watertight bulkheads with access hatches for stowing gear. Some are fitted with pumps for getting rid of water after a capsize. Deck fittings may include recesses for some gear, such as a compass. A sea kayak is ideal for longer journeys and travels easily through rough water. It is less manoeuvreable than normal touring or slalom canoes and therefore less suitable in confined coastal situations and surf.

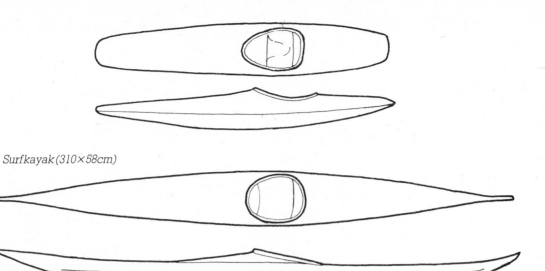

Surfkayak (310×58cm)

Sea kayak (545×54cm)

Below: *Sea kayaks*

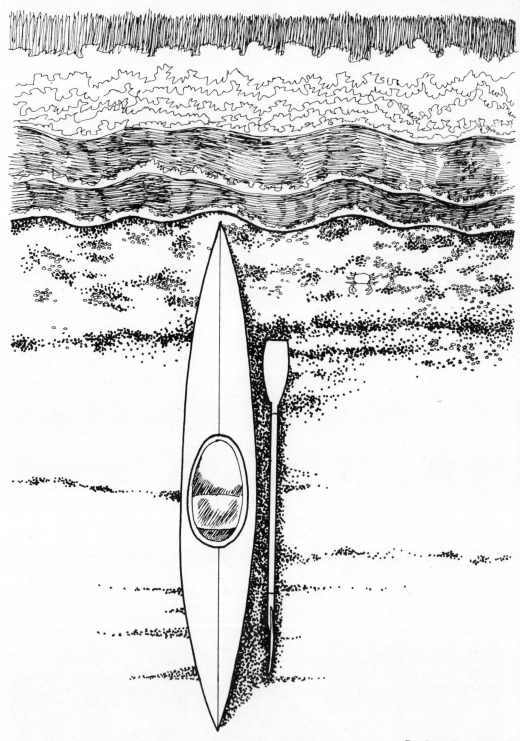

Pre-launch position

Pushing off beach

Surfing

Launching

1 Put your canoe on the beach at right angles to the waves and just clear of the water.
2 Place the paddle beside the canoe. Get in and put on the spraydeck.
3 Using your arms, push and lift yourself and the canoe into the water. Keep the paddle with you. Keep the front of the canoe pointing into the waves or you will be carried back up the beach.
4 As the canoe floats, paddle vigorously out through three or four waves. Keep your chin down and continue to paddle as each wave hits you or again, you will be carried back up the beach.
5 It is tempting to go on paddling out to sea. *Stop*! You may capsize and have a long swim in. Stay in the 'soup' of broken waves close to the shore while you practise a paddle brace.

Paddle brace

1 Turn the canoe sideways to the waves
2 As the wave reaches you lean the canoe towards the wave.
3 Put your paddle blade over the top of the wave, face down, and lean on it. (If the wave is too big to reach over, push the blade through the wave).
4 The movement of the wave will support you. As soon as you feel the wave going away from under you, sit up.
5 Repeat the process with each wave. Larger waves will carry you shorewards.
6 Turn round and practise on the other side.
7 If you lean away from the on coming wave you will capsize very quickly.

Once you can support yourself on either side, paddle out a little further and try to ride in on a wave.

115

Starting to paddle out

Paddling out

Running in

1 Turn the canoe to face the shore. Look over your shoulder, out to sea, and choose a wave.
2 When it is about one canoe length away start paddling forwards.
3 As you feel the stern of the canoe rise on the wave and the canoe accelerate forwards, stop paddling forwards and steer the canoe towards the beach using a stern rudder (see below).

4 Change sides with the paddle as needed to keep travelling towards the beach.
5 At the end of the run, the canoe will turn sideways to the wave.
6 Change quickly to a paddle brace and lean into the wave.
7 Often the canoe will turn away from the side on which you are steering. You must lean very quickly into the turn and get your paddle out of the steering stroke on one side into a paddle brace on the other.

Using stern rudder

Running in

Initially you will find you either start paddling too late and get 'left behind' or that you continue to paddle forwards for too long and race the wave to the beach! Practise will improve your timing. Waves frequently approach the beach at an angle and not parallel. Watch the waves and make sure you line up your canoe to run with the wave. In the diagram (right), the run-in marked with the solid lines could result in the canoe turning left or right.

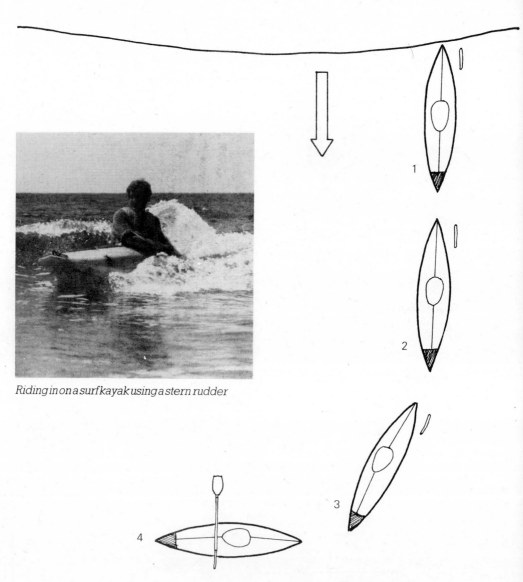

Riding in on a surf kayak using a stern rudder

Running in using a stern rudder (1, 2 and 3), and paddling brace (4)

If, however, you deliberately aim your canoe along the dotted line you can be more certain that the canoe will turn right and you are less likely to make a mistake with the direction of the lean and paddle brace.

Running in backwards

This is perfectly feasible. Practise on very small waves at first and be sure there is no one behind you.

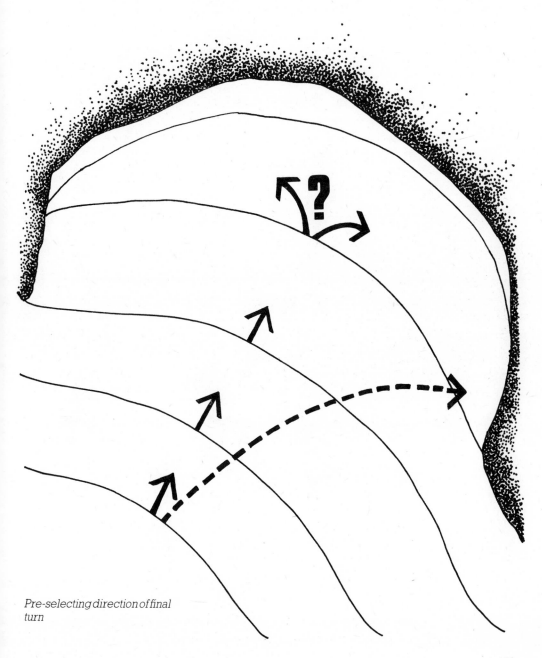

Pre-selecting direction of final turn

Other Manoeuvres in surf

There are many combinations of turns and gymnastics you can learn. Here is one which occasionally happens anyway!

Forward loop

This usually occurs on short, steep waves at the moment the wave starts to 'heap up' before breaking. As the bow of the canoe slides down the face of the wave and dips under the water, the stern stands up into the vertical position and then continues through 180°. This leaves you upside down. Now complete the manoeuvre with an Eskimo roll (page 149) and you are facing back out to sea, ready to go again.

The loop can be encouraged by leaning forward as the bow dips, or discouraged by leaning backwards.

Although many people use slalom canoes for surfing there are specialist surf kayaks now on the market. A cross between a kayak and a malibu board, they are very manoeuvrable and make the best of surf. They are not suitable for general canoeing.

The forward loop

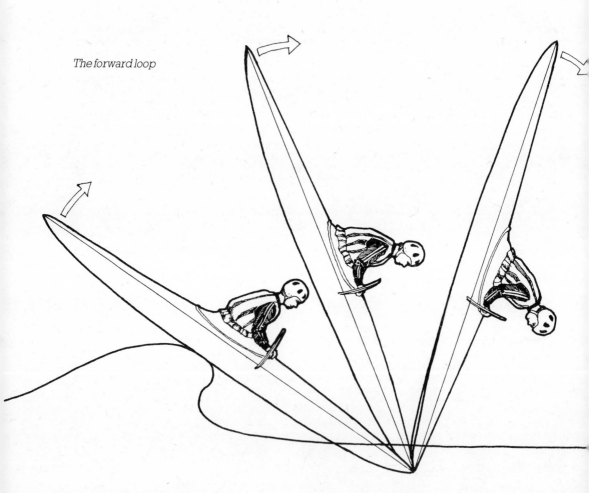

Starting loop (above)
and roll (left and below)

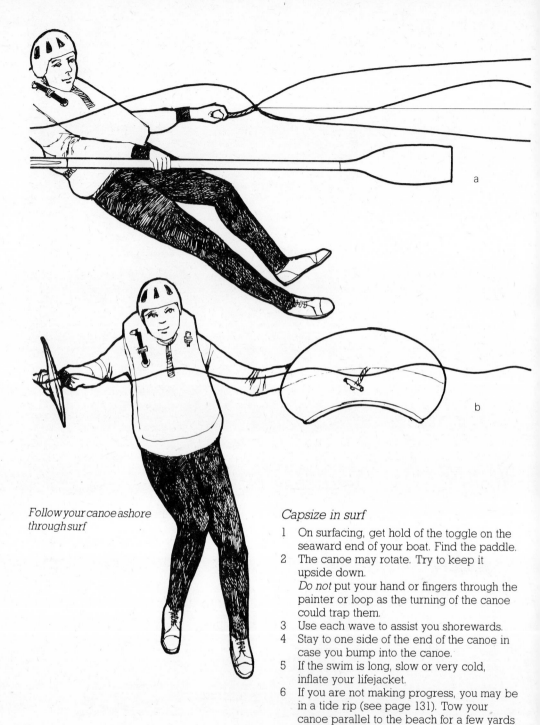

Follow your canoe ashore through surf

Capsize in surf

1 On surfacing, get hold of the toggle on the seaward end of your boat. Find the paddle.
2 The canoe may rotate. Try to keep it upside down.
   Do not put your hand or fingers through the painter or loop as the turning of the canoe could trap them.
3 Use each wave to assist you shorewards.
4 Stay to one side of the end of the canoe in case you bump into the canoe.
5 If the swim is long, slow or very cold, inflate your lifejacket.
6 If you are not making progress, you may be in a tide rip (see page 131). Tow your canoe parallel to the beach for a few yards and try again.
7 Do not attempt deep-water rescues in surf. The risk of collision is too great.

Rock dodging

Emptying canoe

1 When you can stand, float the canoe into shallow water. Stay on the seaward side of it as a canoe full of water is very heavy and could cause injury if pushed against your legs by a wave.
2 Roll the canoe on to its side, cockpit facing the shore. Allow all possible water to run out.
3 See-saw the canoe over your legs to empty completely.

Safety precautions

1 Do not surf alone. Possibly work in pairs, one canoeing, one watching and assisting from the beach.
2 Keep clear of all other people in or on the water. If on a collision course, capsize immediately. The drag of your body in the water will stop the canoe and prevent damage to canoes and people.
3 Check your footrest regularly. Back it up with a solid bulkhead or polystyrene block.
4 Use maximum buoyancy.
5 Wear a lifejacket/buoyancy aid and helmet.
6 Watch your position relative to the shore and do not drift out to sea or along the shore.
7 Be sure you understand the local tides, rip currents and the effect of offshore winds.

Coping with breaking waves

Although the techniques described refer to waves coming ashore on a beach there are several other reasons why waves break, most of which you will experience on a coastal trip or sea crossing. For example, waves may bounce back at you from rocks or cliffs, the wind strength may cause the wave to break or the action of a tide race may do the same. In all cases, your paddle is your balancing aid and rudder and you must use it constantly in rough conditions.

1 If you have to paddle into large, oncoming waves, reach forward through the crest as it approaches and paddle all the time until the steepest part has passed.
2 If the waves are coming from the side, use your legs to hold the canoe and let the boat slide over the wave.
3 Only if the wave breaks do you need to use a paddle brace.
4 If you want to get ashore through breaking waves without surfing in, paddle forwards in the troughs of the waves and backwards as each crest passes under (or over!) you. As the last wave passes, paddle in hard to the beach, riding on the back of the wave.

Paddling strongly in rough sea

To get ashore without surfing
a—paddle forwards
b,c—paddle backwards
d,e,f—paddle forwards
g—arrive on beach on back of wave
h—pull canoe clear before next wave breaks

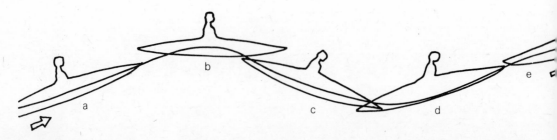

Canoe rides over non-breaking waves

Paddle brace needed if wave breaks

Behaviour of water

The movements of the sea are caused by two major forces, the tide and the wind. A detailed knowledge of both is desirable for at least one member of a group of sea canoeists, but the following simplified information will give you a working knowledge and hopefully, lead you on to further study.

Tidal streams

Tides are caused by the gravitational and centrifugal forces exerted between the sun, the moon and the earth. The earth rotates on its axis once in twenty-four hours. The huge gravitational force of the moon heaps up the waters of the earth on the side nearest the moon and due to centrifugal force at exactly the opposite point, giving two high-water points and a corresponding low-water band. There are three types of tides, probably due to the various physical characteristics of each ocean as well as the movement of the earth. The types are:

1   Semi-diurnal, with two high- and two low-water periods in twenty-four hours, found on the coasts of Britain and Western Europe.
2   Diurnal, with one high- and one low-water period in twenty-four hours, found in and near the tropics.
3   Mixed, with two high- and two low-water periods in twenty-four hours but with marked differences in the heights of successive high and successive low tides, found on the Australian coast, the Pacific coast of North America and the eastern coast of Asia.

The exact timing of semi-diurnal tides is

1   Water flows in or floods for 6 hours 12½ minutes to high water.
2   It then flows out or ebbs for 6 hours 12½ minutes to low water.
3   The sequence is repeated, the total time taken being 24 hours 50 minutes, making the times of high and low water 50 minutes later each day.

4   The water will become still or slack before the tide turns at high or low water. The time of slack water varies, sometimes coinciding with high or low water but more often occurring later, and occasionally earlier, as the volume of water involved in the change causes local differences.
5   Taking the 6 hour period of a flood or ebb tide, in the first and sixth hours the water will flow relatively slowly, in the second and fifth hours more quickly and in the third and fourth hours at its fastest. This can make a great difference to the canoeist, especially where tide races and spring tides are involved.

Spring and neap tides

The earth and moon are in orbit round the more powerful but more distant sun. At the times when the earth, moon and sun are in a straight line, at full and new moon, the force exerted on the waters of the earth is greater than usual and there is more water movement, resulting in higher high-tide levels and lower low-tide levels. These are called spring tides. At the times when the sun and moon are at right angles to each other, in the first and last quarter, the force they exert is lessened and the tidal range is less. These are called neap tides. As the moon takes twenty-eight days to orbit the earth, the state of the tide is governed by this lunar month. The height of the tide will increase or 'make' daily for a week to spring tides and then decrease or 'take-off' for a week to neap tides, when the pattern repeats itself. Further variations in the tidal range occur because the orbit of the moon is elliptical.

Tidal constants

To make the best use of the tide you will need to know which way the water is flowing, the time of high, low and slack water and whether the tides are springs or neaps. This information can be collected from a chart, *Reed's Nautical Almanac* and local tide tables. The coastguard is always able to answer queries you may have. Much abridged tide tables can be bought from chandlery, angling

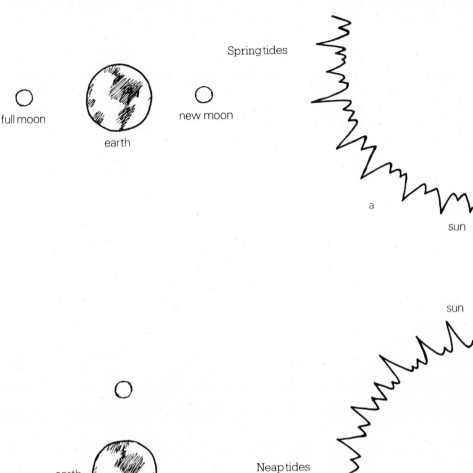

Spring tides

full moon

earth

new moon

a

sun

sun

earth

Neap tides

b

or book shops. The tide tables will be based on the nearest principle port and all the information will refer to that one place. In the front of the booklet there will be a list of more local places. Against each will be the number of hours and/or minutes you must add or subtract to or from the principle port data to correct it to the smaller place. These are called tidal constants.

Local disturbances

Any land mass will interfere with the speed and direction of the main tidal flow. The shape of the coastline will cause currents, races and overfalls which are of special interest to the canoeist. Close to land the sea behaves like a giant river with main and subsidiary streams which a canoeist can use to advantage, travelling with the main stream, ferry gliding across it to outlying islands, or working against it in the eddies and slack water close to land.

Tide Race

Off every prominent headland and on the downstream side (thus changing location when the tide turns) will be faster moving and confused water. This is due to the mainstream hitting the headland and being forced out to sea, where it is stopped by the huge weight of water already there. This causes the water to heap up on the upstream side and then accelerate through the reduced available space. These tide races make good canoeing as long as you understand them. If you find yourself in one accidentally, try ferry gliding clear of the current; failing that, paddle with the current as most tide races are short lived.

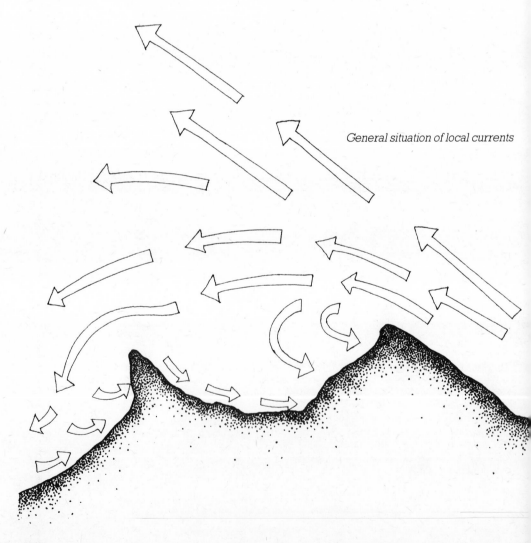

General situation of local currents

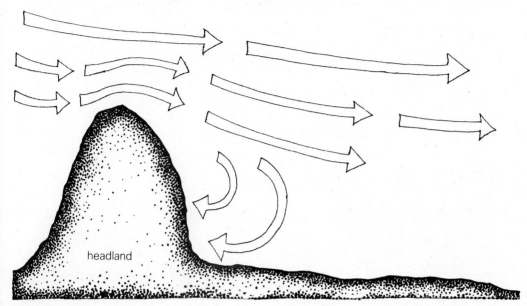

Currents around headland

Tide race

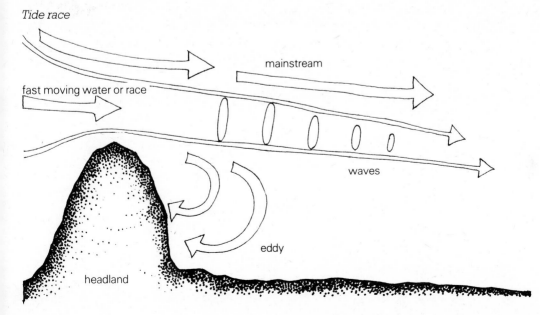

headland

fast moving water or race

mainstream

waves

eddy

headland

Tide race at South Stack

Overfalls

Where the sea becomes shallow suddenly due to sand banks or rock ledges, the water will be forced up and over the obstruction and will produce waves on the surface. These often occur with tide races and will produce very confused conditions. During spring tides, strong winds or a combination of the two, these may become extreme.

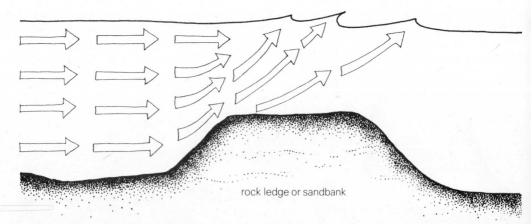

rock ledge or sandbank

In general, tides are predictable, although the times of high or low water can occasionally be advanced or retarded by strong winds. Learn to use the tidetables and seek advice from the coastguard or other informed local people.

Waves

Waves are caused by wind. The stronger the wind, the longer the fetch or distance over the water the wind is blowing, and the longer it blows, the larger the waves will become. Complex air pressure systems over an ocean will create winds of different speeds, directions and ages so that at any one time there will be many wave patterns in existence. Waves will break when the wind strength blows the crest off or when the waves meet an obstruction. Assessing the strength of the wind (see page 167) and obtaining weather forecasts to give advance warning of increasing wind strength or a change of direction is important. The following situations should be recognized.

1 *Wind against tide* produces short, steep waves.
Wind with tide produces longer, flatter waves.

As the tide turns the character of the sea can change dramatically and should be anticipated.

2 Where waves come up against a solid obstruction such as cliffs or a sea wall, they will be deflected back out to sea, creating extra local disturbance as they pass through oncoming waves.

3 Other waves will eventually die out on a beach. Some creating regular lines of surf, others in a chaos of broken waves or 'soup'. Where the beach shelves steeply, the wave will break suddenly from a height and is called a 'dumper'. Canoeists coming ashore must ride in on the back of the wave and once on shore, leap out of the canoe and pull it clear of the water before the next wave arrives.

4 Tide rip. On many beaches there is a naturally low area which acts as a drain to allow water to run back out to sea. This is a rip current and can often be picked out, especially from a high vantage point, as a calm area in otherwise breaking waves, where the outflowing water flattens the incoming waves. A useful route out to sea for the surfing canoeist. To be avoided by swimmers and capsized canoeists.

Wave structure

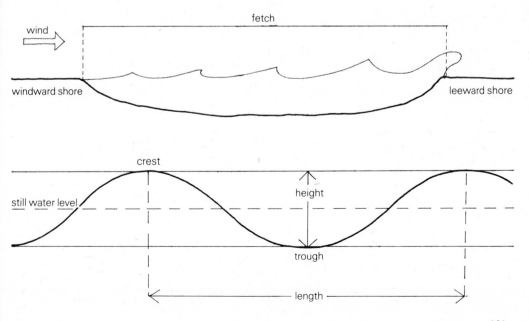

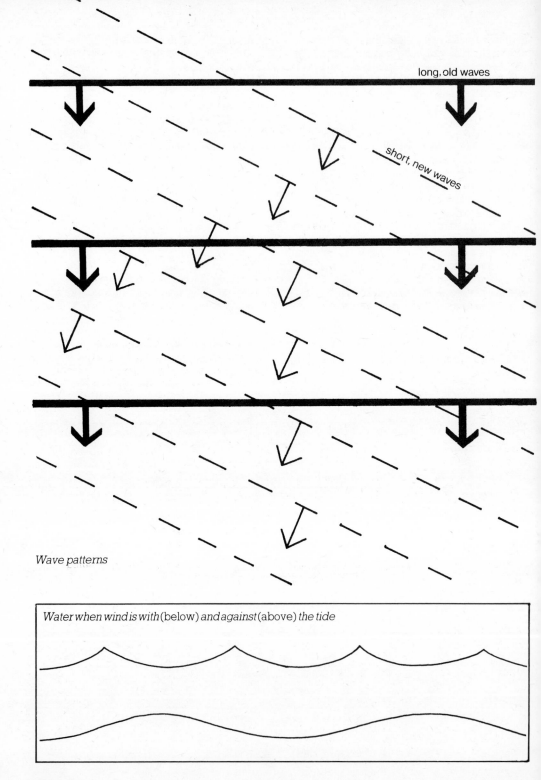

long, old waves

short, new waves

Wave patterns

Water when wind is with (below) and against (above) the tide

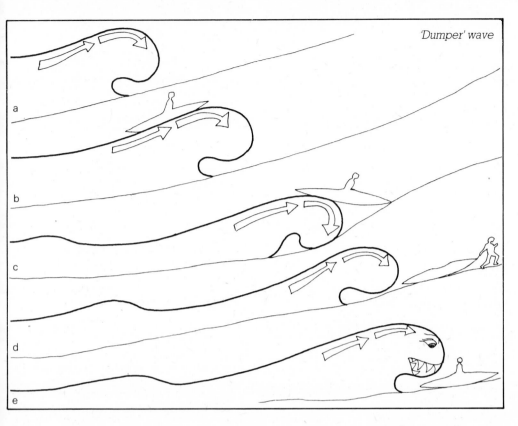

'Dumper' wave

a

b

c

d

e

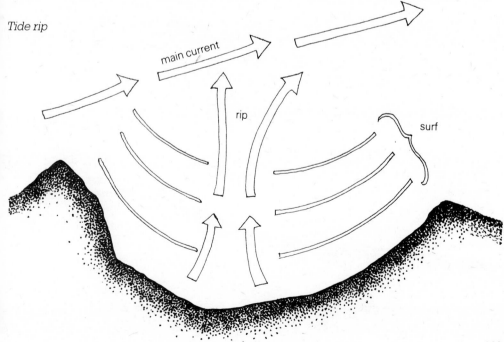

Tide rip

main current

rip

surf

133

5 Estimating wave height. It is usual to overestimate the size of waves when you are on the water and underestimate them while standing on the land, especially if you are standing at some height above the water. Wave height is measured from trough to crest and as you sit in your canoe your eye level will be between 27 and 35 ins./68 and 88 cm. (See also page 131).

6 Onshore winds. As it is usually possible to beach a canoe without damage, onshore winds are only a problem when strong and blowing on to cliffs or rocks. It is essential to have 'escape routes' planned if such conditions are likely.

7 Offshore winds. These will produce a useful, narrow band of protected water. If the winds are strong and the canoeist moves outside the protected area the canoeist could have difficulty in paddling. The capsized canoeist would be in a vulnerable position.

From this information it should be clear that wind speed and direction are most important factors to be considered by the sea canoeist. It is essential that you obtain and interpret correctly a recent weather forecast and make yourself familiar with the signs of approaching bad weather. The Beaufort Wind Scale (page 167) is the one used in forecasts. Force 3 will produce interesting water. Wind of Force 4 and above will interfere with paddling, and produce conditions requiring expert handling.

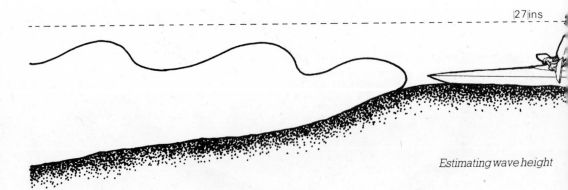

27 ins

Estimating wave height

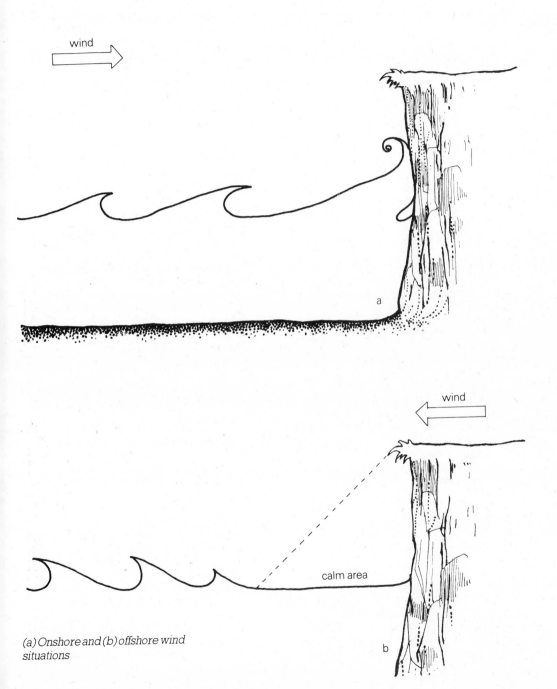

wind

wind

a

calm area

b

(a) Onshore and (b) offshore wind situations

Planning a coastal trip

The group

It is recommended that not less than three or more than about eight people take part. Less than three can make deep-water rescues difficult and more than eight becomes a less manageable unit. Each person should be capable of paddling competently and should have practised deep-water rescues both as patient and rescuer. Within the group, at least one person should be an experienced sea canoeist and take on the leadership of the group. In addition to a suitable canoe with decklines, paddle, personal buoyancy, helmet and spraydeck, each canoeist should carry or wear:

1 Adequate clothing, including hat, sunglasses etc. Some spare clothing and a towel.
2 Food for the day. Spare food for an emergency.
3 Hot drink.
4 6 by 4 foot (1.8 by 1.2 metre) thick-gauge polythene bag for use as an emergency shelter.
5 Whistle.*
6 Large sponge (kept under canoe seat).

In addition the following items should be carried within the group:

1 Waterproof watch.*
2 Map/chart with tide and weather information and compass bearings written out on it.
3 Spare paddles.*
4 First aid kit (see page 169).
5 Canoe repair kit (see page 170).
6 Torch.
7 Compass.*
8 Matches/lighter.
9 Flares.*
10 Knife.*

Those marked * should be carried on the canoe or canoeist. The others should be packed in suitable waterproof containers inside the canoe. Small items such as snack foods, sunglasses, flares, compass, etc. can be carried in pockets on lifejacket or anorak.

The route

1 Buy a map, 1:25,000 or 1:50,000 of the area. Pick out an interesting piece of coast, with access for vehicles and canoes and possible alternative routes for bad weather.
2 Distance. Build up distance gradually. It is better to underestimate your capabilities and there are many interesting things to explore on the way. 5 to 6 miles/ 8 to 10 km could be enough for a first trip, building up to 15 to 20 miles/24 to 32 km and beyond. Strong winds can make an enormous difference to your rate of progress.
3 Tides. Work out the times of high, low and slack water. Plan to work the tides; that is, travel with them. Paddle C to A if the tide is ebbing throughout the trip or A to C if it is flooding. If high water occurs around mid-day, paddle A to B and back to A.
4 Charts. Admiralty and similar charts will show you: depth of water; speed in knots of the flood and ebb tides in the area (a knot is one nautical mile or 6080 feet per hour); nature of sea bed and coast line (sand, rock, cliff, etc.); position of races, overfalls and other local peculiarities; shipping lanes.

Try to get, or look at (the coastguard may help) a chart and mark in on your map relevant details. A booklet explaining symbols used on Admiralty charts can be bought, with the charts, from ships' chandlers.

5 Pilot books. Admiralty pilot books are world wide. They give all relevant information for planning major sea crossings as well as coastal information. Can be bought from chandlers and major bookshops or borrowed from Public Libraries.
6 Navigation. On a coastal trip this consists of route-finding using your map. It is advisable to work out bearings (page 167) for any sections to off-shore islands or where you may be some distance from land. Bad visibility can develop very quickly. All the bearings plus tidal and weather information should be written or drawn in on the map. This is then covered and stuck to the deck of the canoe with a

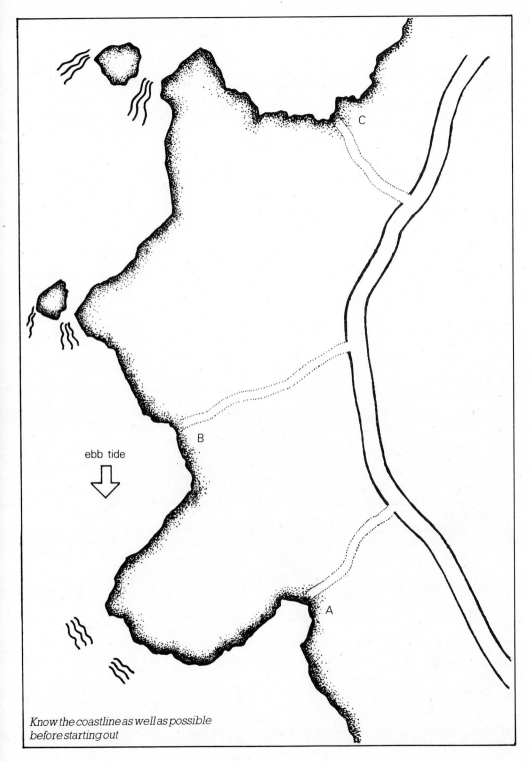

ebb tide

C

B

A

*Know the coastline as well as possible
before starting out*

self adhesive, waterproof and transparent covering. Using a chinagraph pencil you can also make notes on this during the trip. Navigating from a canoe is severely limited by the size and restrictions of the boat. The majority of the calculations must be worked out before going afloat.

Compass

For coastal touring an orienteering compass incorporating magnetic needle, protractor and ruler is adequate. It is relatively robust, lightweight and inexpensive. It can be used for working out a bearing on which to paddle, establishing your exact position when you can see the coast, and to a limited degree paddling on a bearing in poor visibility. For longer sea passages, a small steering compass can be mounted in a recess in the deck and a small bearing compass carried round the neck. It is essential to carry and be able to use the compass of your choice on sea trips.

The day before get a general weather forecast. Assess the situation. Be prepared to abandon or modify the proposed route if the report is unfavourable.

On the day telephone the Coastguard. Ask for the wind speed and direction and state of the sea. Also for any changes expected in the weather. Check with the coastguard that your tidal predictions are correct. If you decide to go ahead with the trip tell the coastguard your name, number of canoeists involved, proposed route, emergency gear carried and expected time of arrival at your destination.

At the end of the day telephone the coastguard again and inform him that you are off the water.

Rescue practice at sea

Preparing for a coastal trip

Emergency procedures

If, in spite of all your planning, something goes wrong make every effort to keep the group together. In the event of a capsize close to rocks, inside caves or other confined spaces where there is a danger of canoes being damaged, the patient should tow his canoe out to more suitable water before the rescue is started. If in a tide race, the patient may be able to tow the canoe into an eddy. Failure to perform a rescue can be serious. In this event, raft up round the capsized canoe and get the patient out of the water on to the raft. Stay in physical contact with each other and set about summoning help – do not delay. Recognized signals are:

1 Use of whistle (not far reaching).
2 Waving of garments tied to paddle.
3 Use of flares; these should be red and project stars or smoke.

Red dye in the water is also an excellent aid to searchers.

The coastguard is the co-ordinator of rescue services. Assuming you have informed him of your plans he will initiate a search if you fail to arrive. Other observers may also report your signals. In the meantime, keep together.

Legal aspects

Tidal water is available for canoeing. The only problem may be access. Parts of the foreshore may be considered private and land leading to the shore often is private. Try to use public access points if there is any doubt.

Some harbour authorities may charge launching and landing fees. These can usually be avoided by moving outside the immediate area of harbour or quay.

There is a lot to learn about the sea before you get the full rewards but these are well worth the effort involved.

Opposite: *Further sea rescue drill*

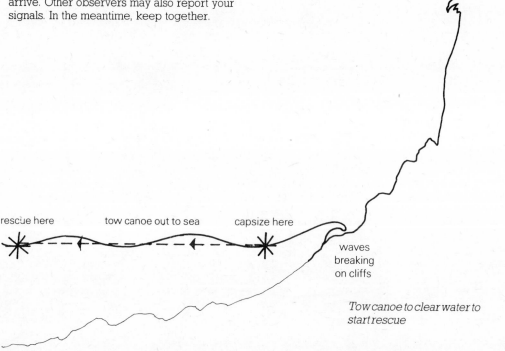

rescue here   tow canoe out to sea   capsize here

waves breaking on cliffs

Tow canoe to clear water to start rescue

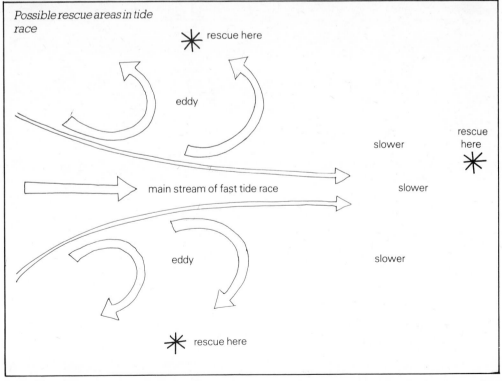

Possible rescue areas in tide race

✳ rescue here

eddy

slower

rescue here ✳

main stream of fast tide race

slower

eddy

slower

✳ rescue here

Chapter Seven
Advanced Techniques

As a canoeist gains experience in the use of
the basic techniques already described, he or
she will learn to put together a series of basic
strokes to deal with a particular piece of
water. It is the ability of the canoeist to read
the water correctly and in sufficient time to
select the right sequence of strokes, that
constitutes advanced techniques. Three
additional strokes are involved.

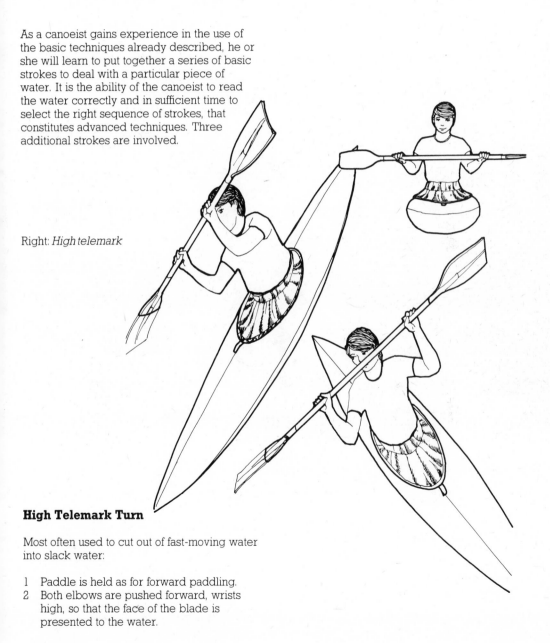

Right: *High telemark*

High Telemark Turn

Most often used to cut out of fast-moving water
into slack water:

1 Paddle is held as for forward paddling.
2 Both elbows are pushed forward, wrists
  high, so that the face of the blade is
  presented to the water.

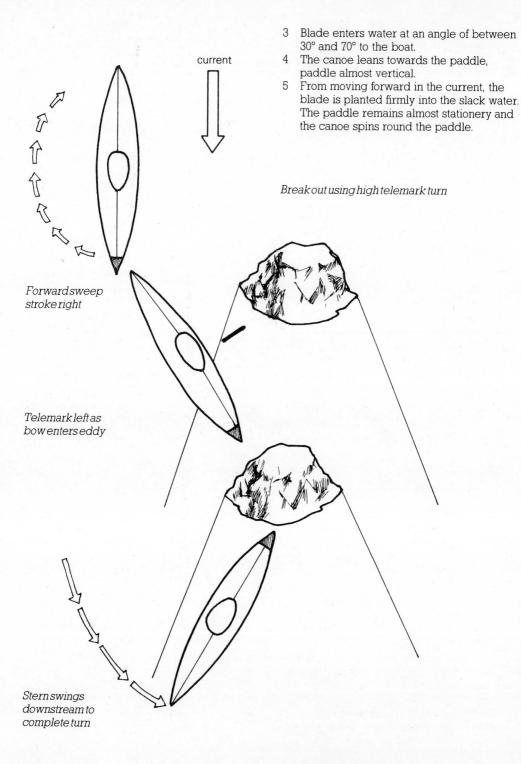

3 Blade enters water at an angle of between 30° and 70° to the boat.
4 The canoe leans towards the paddle, paddle almost vertical.
5 From moving forward in the current, the blade is planted firmly into the slack water. The paddle remains almost stationery and the canoe spins round the paddle.

current

Break out using high telemark turn

Forward sweep stroke right

Telemark left as bow enters eddy

Stern swings downstream to complete turn

Bow rudder

A further turning stroke used for a small but
accurate change of direction. Usually followed
immediately by a forward paddling stroke
without taking the blade out of the water. The
first stroke moves the boat diagonally towards
the blade and the forward paddle stroke
straightens the boat and continues forward
propulsion.

1 Paddle held as for high telemark.
2 Canoeist leans well forward, plants paddle
   as far forward as possible, face towards the
   boat and holds blade firmly until enough
   turn is achieved.
3 Roll the blade over and make a forward
   paddle stroke.

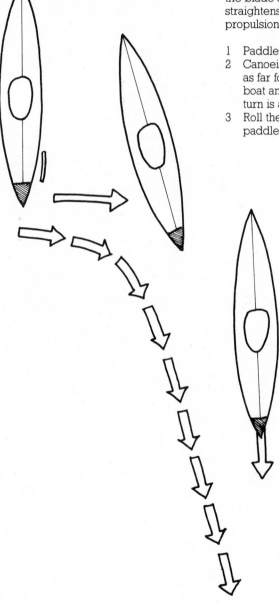

*Forward diagonal
movement using bow
rudder*

Above: *Bow rudder*

Below: *Firm paddling control is required*

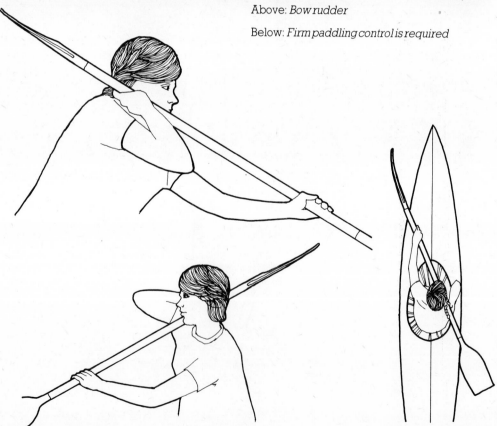

Scull for support

Used when support is needed for a longer time than is given by slap for support.

1   Hold paddle as for forward paddling.
2   Push elbows forward with wrists extended so that the concave face of the blade is down on the water and away from the side of the canoe.
3   Blade now moves to and fro, or sculls, on the surface of the water, parallel to the canoe.
4   At the end of the each scull, the blade angle must change so that the leading edge is always raised.
5   The canoe leans over towards the paddle.
6   To sit up, push down sharply on the blade and use the knees.

Once you are familiar with the various strokes, you will be able to link them together into a sequence. Every canoeist develops favourite combination strokes for dealing with specific situations.

Early stages in learning sculling

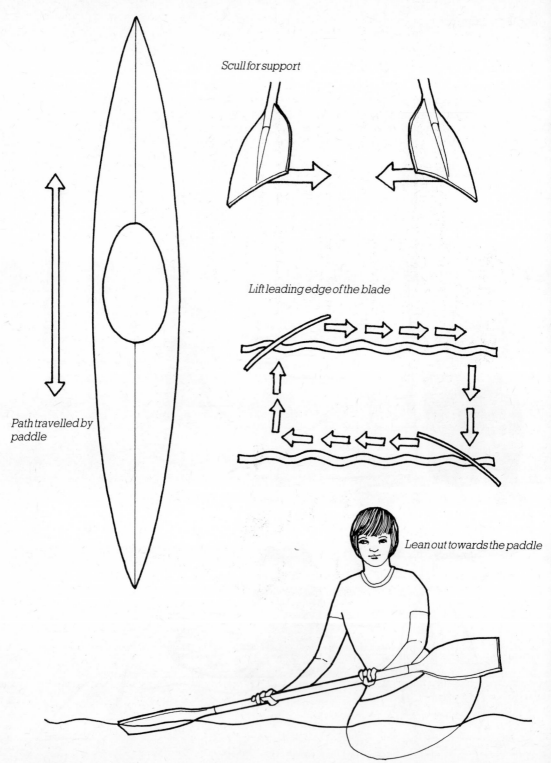

Scull for support

Lift leading edge of the blade

Path travelled by paddle

Lean out towards the paddle

Eskimo roll

The ultimate recovery stroke. The paddle is used as a temporary support on the water while the canoe is turned back up from the capsized position with the legs. Try to get the use of a heated swimming pool and be thoroughly practised in the capsize drill and basic paddling. The canoe used must be a good fit and the footrest correctly adjusted.

Lead-up exercises

1 Sit in canoe, right side to edge of pool. Put both hands, finger tips only, on the pool side (a).
2 Lower yourself under the water until canoe is completely upside down (b).
3 Keep your fingers on the pool side but move them behind you.

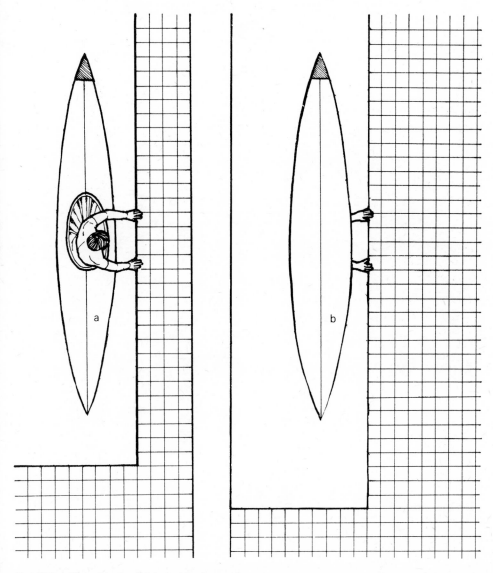

Practising the eskimo roll in a swimming pool

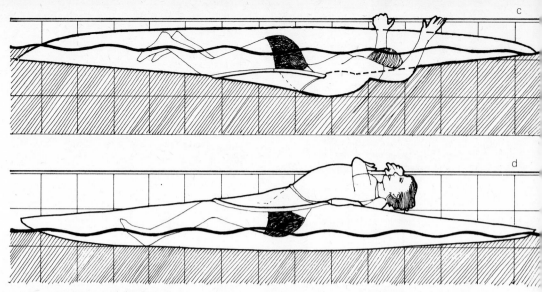

Use the legs to turn the canoe

Stages of the eskimo roll

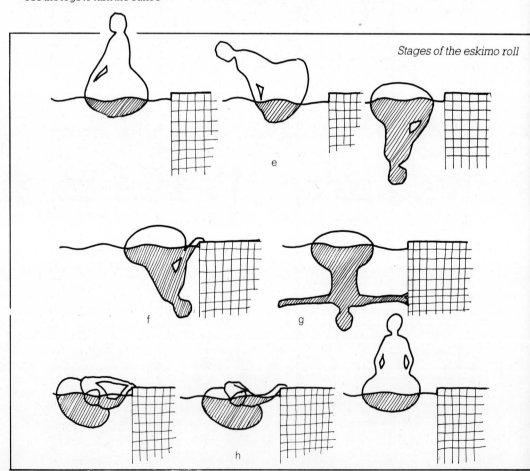

4　Lie back along deck of canoe and to the left side of it (c).
5　Push your left knee hard up under the deck and roll the canoe upright (d).
6　Very little work should be done with the arms.
7　Keep your head on the back deck until the canoe is upright. This keeps your centre of gravity near the centre of gravity of the canoe and helps the boat roll easily. Your body will also create less drag in the water in this position. Practise 1–7 until you can right the canoe putting little weight on your arms.

8　Now lean forward and capsize to the left (e).
9　Reach up on to the pool side on the right with both hands (f). If you become disorientated, stretch both hands out to locate pool side (g).
10　Lie back, head on deck.
11　Roll the canoe (h).

You should now be well orientated and using the legs, called 'hip flick,' to right the canoe. There are several methods of using the paddle to complete the roll; the one described is called 'Pawlata'.

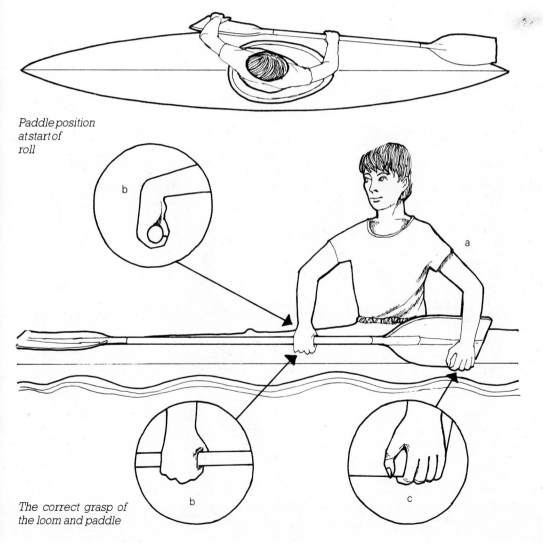

Paddle position at start of roll

The correct grasp of the loom and paddle

Paddle control

1 Hold the paddle along the left deck.
   Forward blade face up, rear blade vertical.
2 Right hand holds loom – wrist fully flexed.
3 Left hand holds rear blade. Fingers and
   thumb on the outside grasping lower
   corner. Hands a comfortable width apart.
4 Hold paddle very firmly in position.
   Now get one or two people to help. Move
   well away from pool side. Helpers stand on
   your left (a).
5 Capsize left towards your helpers. Lean
   forward (b and c).
6 Do not move. Sit still in the kayak and
   check that the right paddle blade is still in
   contact with the front deck and the right
   wrist is fully flexed or cocked (d).
7 The two helpers now right the canoe by
   reaching over the hull and pulling on the
   left side of the canoe (e).

Practising with a companion

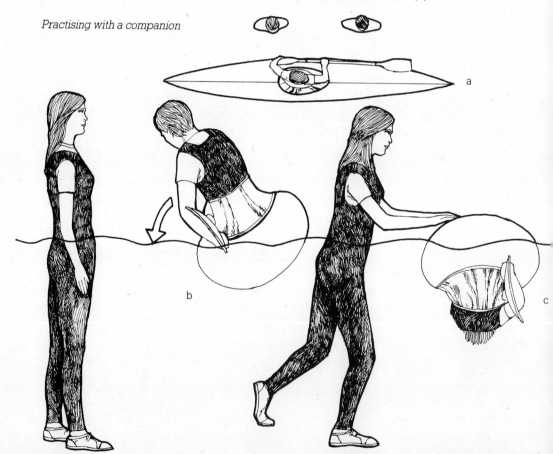

152

Practise this until you are happy to sit
upside-down eyes open and check the
position of your wrist and paddle.

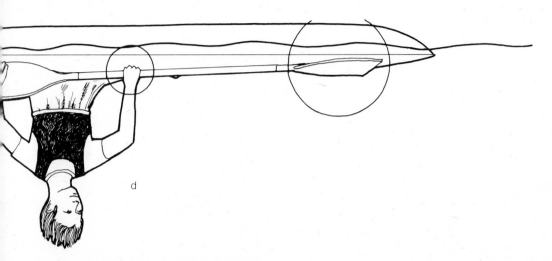

d

*Learn to get used to being upside
down for short periods*

e

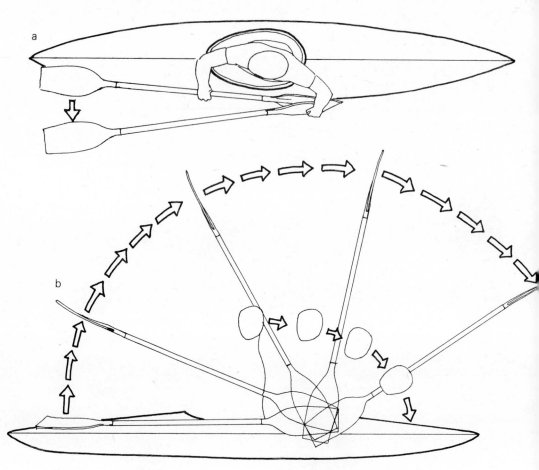

Paddle stroke

Practise this, sitting upright in the canoe.
1 Place the paddle in position.
2 From the deck, push the right blade away from the canoe to the left as far as you can reach. Lead off with the cocked wrist. This sets the correct blade angle (a).
3 Now let the wrist unwind as you sweep the blade in a half circle over your head, allowing your body to move back on to the back deck (b).

Rear view of starting position

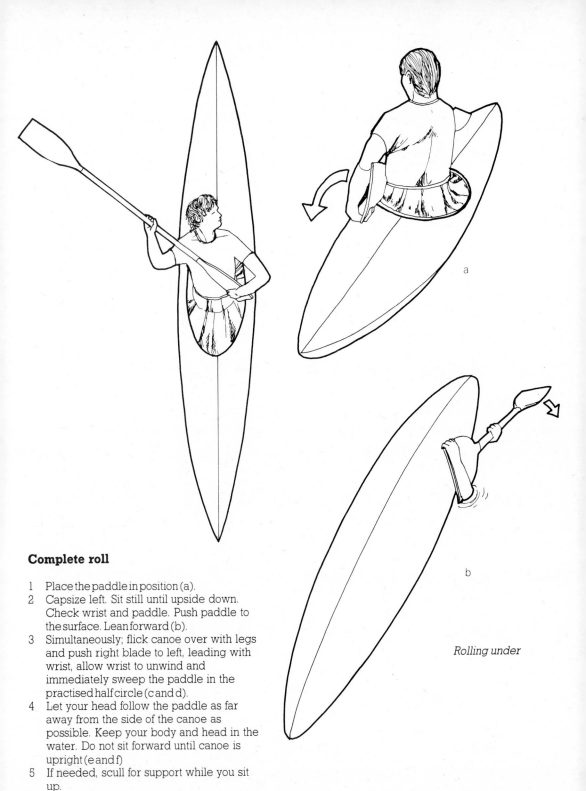

Rolling under

Complete roll

1 Place the paddle in position (a).
2 Capsize left. Sit still until upside down. Check wrist and paddle. Push paddle to the surface. Lean forward (b).
3 Simultaneously; flick canoe over with legs and push right blade to left, leading with wrist, allow wrist to unwind and immediately sweep the paddle in the practised half circle (c and d).
4 Let your head follow the paddle as far away from the side of the canoe as possible. Keep your body and head in the water. Do not sit forward until canoe is upright (e and f)
5 If needed, scull for support while you sit up.

155

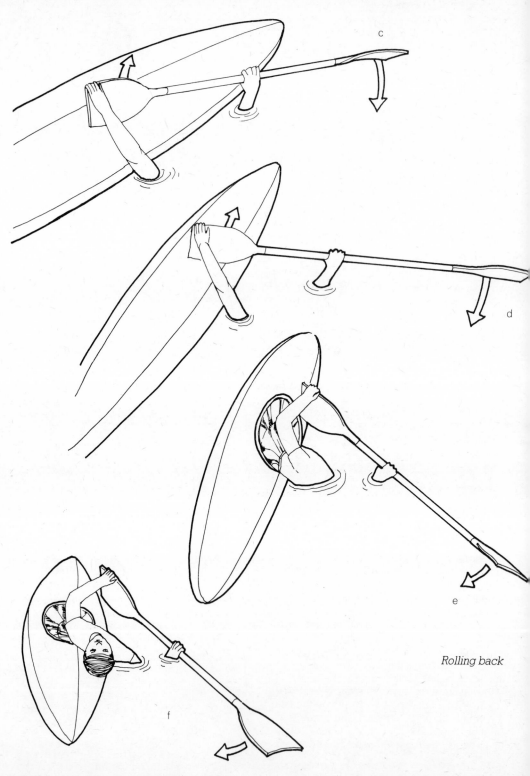

c

d

e

Rolling back

f

The Eskimo roll is not difficult but it requires some degree of accuracy and good timing. Professional instruction in a pool is the best way of learning but these notes may help. Once you can roll, capsize in the forward paddling position and line up your paddle under water. Then start the whole sequence again on the other side. Finally, the roll can be achieved when holding the paddle as for forward paddling. Called the screw roll it has the great advantage of needing little under water preparation as the hands are already in position.

The screw roll starting position

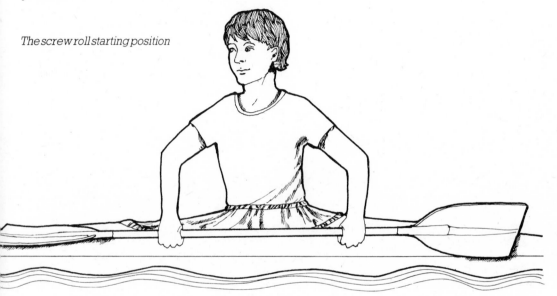

Eskimo rescue

This is an assisted rescue, only possible if the patient has confidence to wait, upside down, to be rescued. Practise the leg work or 'hip flick' as in the Eskimo roll.

1 Capsized patient remains in canoe. Attracts attention by banging on bottom of boat (a).
2 Moves hands slowly backwards and forwards along both sides of canoe, giving rescuer larger area to aim for (b and c).
3 Rescuer paddles along side and places bow of his canoe gently into patient's hand (d).
4 Patient transfers both hands to bow, lies back and flicks canoe upright (e, f and g).
5 Alternatively the rescuer can place his paddle over the two parallel canoes and help the patient grasp the loom whilst righting the canoe (h).
6 Always feel for the rescuer with a hand on either side of the canoe; your boat may have spun round during the capsize.

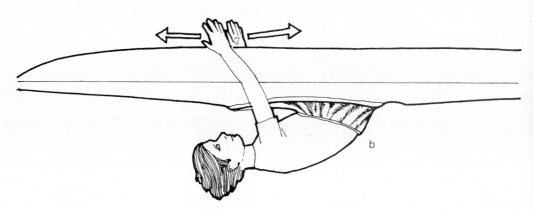

Techniques of eskimo rescue

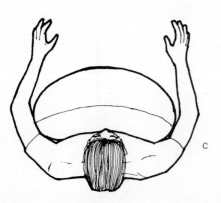

Advanced techniques develop with personal practice and experience and by canoeing in the company of more experienced canoeists than yourself.

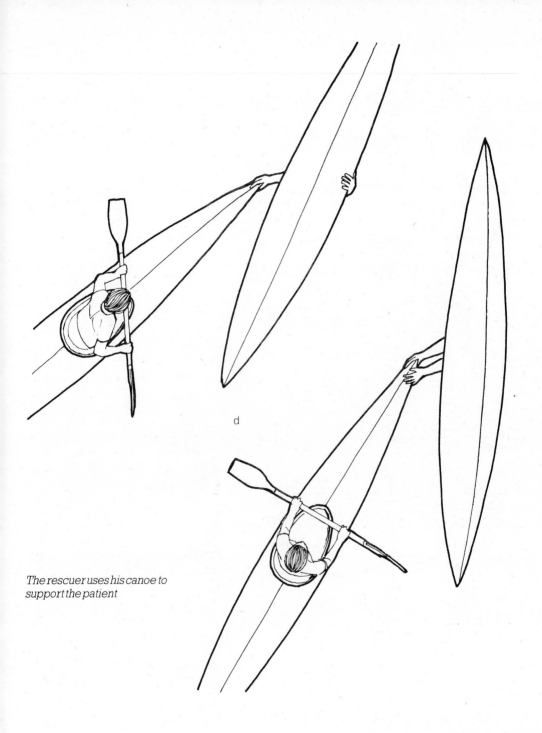

d

The rescuer uses his canoe to support the patient

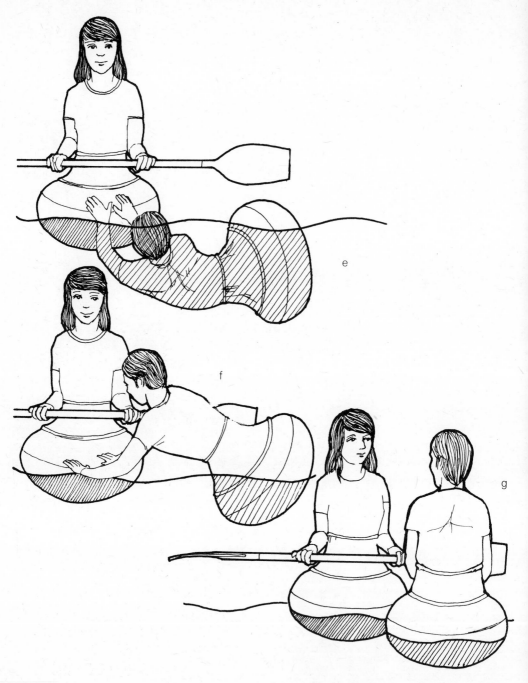

e

f

g

Use hip-flick to complete eskimo rescue

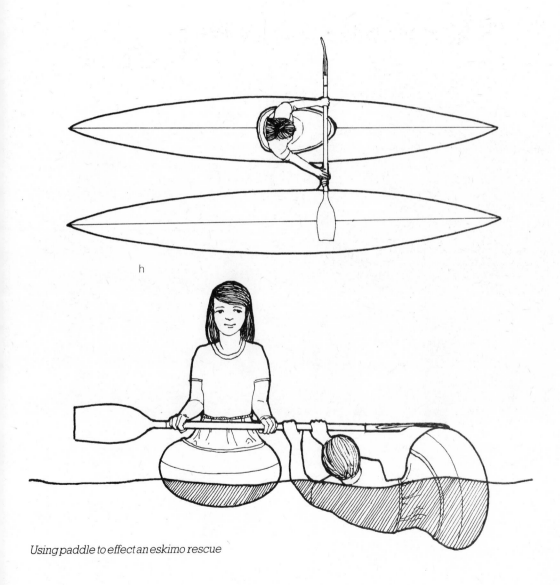

h

Using paddle to effect an eskimo rescue

Chapter Eight
Expeditions by Canoe

The main difference between a canoe-camping tour and an expedition is the objective of the journey. Many touring canoeists travel abroad to a different country in pursuit of a good holiday; the expedition canoeist is searching for a new challenge which may be the first descent of a giant Himalayan river, the crossing of an ocean or the exploration of remote wilderness. Generally speaking, major expeditions are outside the scope of this book, but an outline of the considerations is included to demonstrate the potential of journeys by kayak.

It is assumed that such an expedition would be to a remote area, and therefore independent and outside the assistance of the usual medical and rescue services.

Most canoe expeditions are initiated by a small group of canoeists who agree on an objective. From that moment on it may take from one to two years to finalise the plans. The following list is suggested as a possible scheme of work during the planning period:

1 Decide on the objective.
2 Study the climatic conditions of the area concerned and plan the most suitable time for the attempt.
3 Apply to all relevant government authorities for permission to travel across the countries and proceed with the objective. This can take many months and still end in last minute refusals. It is wise to have a second plan ready when it is known that this situation could occur.
4 Raise funds. Many organisations and firms will give money, goods, or cost price equipment to an interesting venture and all approaches must be made in good time. It should be understood that in return you may have to produce an official

expedition report or suitable advertising material.
5 Transport will be the most expensive item. Canoes have been carried in 'planes, and as hand luggage on a ship. Cars or minibus should also be considered. Money and time available will decide the issue for you, but consider all the possibilities.
6 At this stage it is worth writing to any contacts you may have in or 'en route' for the area. Local people can often prevent problems arising or sort them out quickly.
7 Purchase or make all necessary equipment as early as possible. Tests, trials and alterations take time. A pre-expedition trip would be invaluable if circumstances permit. This gives team members a chance to try out gear and work together as a group.
8 You will need the best available maps, charts and guides. Many will be old and inaccurate which may give ideas for future trips.
9 Dried food is probably the most common type to be used on expeditions. It is light in weight, does not deteriorate quickly and is not too bulky. It is relatively palatable for short periods of time. It does require supplies of fresh water. A variety of food stuffs, including some small luxury items, is essential and the whole diet must be well balanced if the team is to remain healthy. In some cases, fresh food may be bought during the trip and, if not all the food can be carried in the boats, arrangements must be made to re-stock, possibly by using advance food dumps. The cost of doing this would be high. Fishing is an excellent way of supplementing the diet and can be effectively combined with canoeing. It is worth the time spent to split all foodstuffs into packs, e.g. 2 man – 1 day, etc. and waterproof each pack. Food is

easily contaminated. In transit and in boats, keep your food at maximum distance from petrol, paraffin, resin etc.

10   When travelling in remote places illness or accident could prove serious or even fatal. It is wise to take every precaution before setting off. Visit your dentist and doctor for a check up and any necessary innoculations. At least one member of the team should have advanced first aid experience and should, with the assistance of a qualified medical adviser, put together a comprehensive first aid kit. Apart from obvious precautions with hygiene and drinking water (upset stomachs are common) use of mosquito-proof tents may be necessary.

11   Even in a very remote area it may be possible to get help in an emergency. This type of cover must be arranged in advance. It may be possible to pre-arrange a regular rendez-vous time or carry a small radio beacon which, when activated, transmits an emergency signal.

12   To cope with a situation of totally hopeless weather conditions, illness or accident, the quickest ways out of the area from given points, should be studied in advance. It is much easier, when faced with a decision to abandon the objective, if escape routes are already planned.

13   Fuel supplies for cooking can often be supplemented by open fires from driftwood etc. If not, then fuel will have to be used sparingly and stocks replenished when possible. Advance fuel dumps could be set up.

14   During a long expedition it is essential to plan regular rest days. In one recent sea expedition it was found that 60 miles (100 km) in three days followed by a rest day, was acceptable. On a major white-water river expedition in the Himalaya distances sometimes dropped to as little as 4 miles (6 km) a day. You must be as flexible as possible and allow for the unexpected.

15   Insurance is essential. Find out about the type of medical and rescue facilities available and how much they might cost.

16   After the expedition is over there will still be work to be done. Many people must be informed of the outcome and many thanked for their help. Probably one of the least interesting aspects of the trip, it is well worth doing thoroughly and quickly if you and others are to be supported on future occasions. It is often possible to add to expedition funds by giving slide lectures, producing a film or a book.

One thing is certain, once you have been involved in a successful expedition you will be planning the next before you reach home.

Chapter Nine
Useful Information

1 International Canoe Federation – affiliated members

Argentina Federacion Argentina de Canoas, Florida 229, 3° piso – of. 332, Buenos Aires.

Australia Australian Canoe Association, c/o P. J. Thompson, 30 Melaleca, Carrum 3197, Melbourne.

Austria Österreichischischer Kanu-Verband, Bergganse 16, 1090 Wien Tel. (0222) 349203. Cable: OE-Kanu Wien.

Belgium Federation Belge de Canoe, Belgisch Kano Verbond, c/o A. Vandeput, Geerdengemwaart 79, B. 2800, Mechelen. Tel. (015) 415459.

Bulgaria Bulgarian Canoe Federation, Bulevar Tolboukine 18, Sofia. Cable: Besefese-Sofia – tel. 8651. Telex 22723–22723.

Canada Canadian Canoe Association, 333 River Road, Place Vanier, Vanier City, Ontario K1L 8B9. Tel. (613) 746–0060. Telex 053–3660.

Cyprus Cyprus Canoe Association, P.O. Box 1384, Nicosia.

Cuba Federation Cubana de Canotaje, c/o Comite Olimpico Cubano, Hotel Habana Libre, La Habana

Czechoslovakia Czechoslovak Canoe Federation, Na porici 12, 11530 Praha 1. Cable: Sportsvaz-Praha – Tel. 249541–9. Telex cstv c 122650.

DPR of Korea Canoe Association of the Democratic People's, Moosing-Dong, Dongdawon District, Pyongyang.

Denmark Dansk Kano og Kajak Forbund, c/o J. Cronberg, Engvej 184–2300 Copenhagen S. Cable: Dancasport Copenhagen. Tel. (01) 554509.

Federal Republic of Germany DeutscherKanu-Verband, Berta-Allee 8, 4100 Duisburg 1. Tel. (0203) 72965/72966.

Finland Suomen Kanoottiliitto ry, Topeliuksenkatu 41a, 00250 Helsinki 25.

France Federation Francaise de Canoe-Kayak, 87 Quai de la Marne, 94, 340 Joinville Le Pont.Tel. 873.79.25.

German Democratic Republic Deutscher Kanu-Sport-Verband. Storkowerstr. 118, 1055 Berlin. Cable: DTSB (Kanusport) Berlin. Tel. 4384342/4384396.

Great Britain British Canoe Union, Flexel House, 45/47 High Street, Addlestone, Weybridge, Surrey, KT15 1JV. Tel. Weybridge (97) 41341.

Hong Kong Hong Kong Canoe Union, Room 502, Mau Wai Commercial Building, 102 Wellington Street, Central Hong Kong.

Hungary Magyar Kajak-Kanu Szövetseg, Rosenberg Hazuspar u. 1, Budapest V. Cable: Comsport Kayak-Budapest. Tel. 114.800.

Iran Iranian Rowing and Water Ski Federation, Kakh Varzesh str. P.O. Box 3396, Teheran.

Ireland Irish Canoe Union, c/o Cospoir The National Sport Council, Floor 11, Hawkins House, Hawkins Street, Dublin 2.

Israel Israel Canoe Association, 8 Haarbaa Street, P.O.B. 7170, Tel-Aviv. Tel. 26.01.81.5

Italy Commissione Italiana Canoa, Viale Tiziano 70, 00100 Roma. Tel. 36851.

Ivory Coast Ivory Coast Canoes and Pirogue Federation, B.P. 1872, Abidjan.

Japan Japan Canoe Association, c/o Kishi Memorial 1 – 1 – 1 Jinnan Shibuya-ku, Tokyo. Cable: JAAA Tokyo 'Kanoe.' Tel. 3–467–6794.

Luxembourg Federation Luxembourgeoise de Canoe-Kayak, Boite postale 424, Luxembourg 2. Tel. 29155.

Mexico Federation Mexicana de Canotaje, Sanchez Ascona 1348, Mexico 12, D.F. Tel. 575.15.60/575.13.65.

Netherlands Nederlandse Kano Bond, Central Bureau, N.B., Henri Dunanstraat 62, 1561 Bd Krommenie.

New Zealand New Zealand Canoeing Association Inc., P.O. Box 5125, Auckland.

Norway Norges Kajak-Forbund, Hauger Skolovei 1, N. 1346 Gjettum.

People's Republic of China Canoeing Association of the People's Republic of China, 9 Tiyukuan Road, Peking. Cable: Sportschine Peking.

Poland Polski Zwiszek Kajakowy, ul. Sienkiewicza 12, 00–010 Warszawa. Cable: Kajak-Warszawa. Tel. 27.49.16.

Romania Federatia Romana de Caiac-Canoe, Str. Vasile Conta 16, 70139 Bucarest. Tel. 119787. Telex 11180. Cable: Sportrom-Bucarest.

Soviet Union Canoe Federation of the U.S.S.R., Skaternyi pereoulok 4, Moscow 69. Cable: Sportkomitet Moscow. Tel. 2903940.

Spain Federcion Espagnola de Piragüismo, c/o Miguel Angel, num. 18, 6°Madrid 10 Tel. 4103815/4104048.

Sweden Svenska Kanotförbundet, Idrottens Hus, 123 87 Farsta. Tel. 08–930500.

Switzerland Schweizerischer Kanu-Varband, c/o Frau G. Vogler-Lintner, Brunigstrasse 121, 6060 Sarnen. Tel. 041 66.34.88.

USA American Canoe Association, National Office, P.O. Box 242, Lorton, Virginia 22079.

Yugoslavia Kajakaski Savez Jugoslavije, Bulevar Revolucije 44/I, 11000 Beograd. Cable: Kajak Beograd.

South Africa South African Canoe Association, c/o W. F. van Riet, 13 Leopold Street, Bellville. (Suspended by the 1970 Congress in Copenhagen.)

2 Weather

The weather, particularly a sudden deterioration, is probably the most serious single factor to threaten the safety of canoeists, particularly on large lakes, estuaries and the sea. If you have no experience of weather observation and interpretation, you must first learn to use the information gathered together by the expert. Do not wait until you are about to use the information in earnest, start practising now:

1 Familiarize yourself with the forecast areas.
2 Watch and listen to weather forecasts, particularly shipping and coastal ones, on a regular basis. Write down the general synopsis, the forecast for your own area and the report from your nearest weather station.

3 If possible, obtain current weather map (synoptic chart) from the daily paper.
4 Take particular note of th speed and direction of movement of depressions or low-pressure areas; they bring bad or unsettled weather. They could be 'deepening' (pressure falling still further) or 'filling' (pressure rising).
5 A depression may have associated with it, warm, cold or occluded fronts which will further disturb the weather pattern.
6 Falling pressure, especially if rapidly falling, indicates bad weather.
7 Note the Beaufort wind scale number and wind direction. Wind blows anti-clockwise in a depression in the northern hemisphere and clockwise in the southern hemisphere.
8 Having obtained the official forecasts and synoptic chart, observe the actual timing of events throughout the day, e.g. a front approaching or changes of wind direction as high or low pressure areas move. Try and relate them to the information obtained and make notes of your observations. In time, you will become proficient at estimating the type of weather which will arrive following a given forecast. Back this up with some further reading.

All this assumes that you are able to obtain official forecasts. This is one good reason for taking a small radio receiver on longer trips. If you have to rely on your own observations you will need to make a more detailed study of weather forecasting including cloud formation. A barometer for measuring the air pressure would be extremely useful.

3 International sea-scale

Number	Description of sea	Wave height crest to trough (feet)
0	calm	0
1	smooth	0 – ½
2	light	½ – 2
3	moderate	2 – 5
4	rough	5 – 9
5	very rough	9 – 15
6	high	15 – 24
7	very high	24 – 36
8	precipitous	36 +

4 Beaufort Scale of wind force

Beauford number	Limits of wind speed in (knots)	Description	Sea state	Probable height of waves in (feet)
0	less than 1	calm	sea like a mirror	–
1	1 – 3	light air	ripples	–
2	4 – 6	light breeze	small wavelets	½
3	7 – 10	gentle breeze	large wavelets: occasional white horses	2
4	11 – 16	moderate breeze	small waves: some white horses	3½
5	17 – 21	fresh breeze	moderate waves: many white horses	6
6	22 – 27	strong breeze	large waves: extensive white crests	9½
7	28 – 33	near gale	white foam from breaking waves	13½
8	34 – 40	gale	moderately high waves of greater length	18
9	41 – 47	strong gale	high waves: crests tumble: much spray	23
10	48 – 55	storm	very high waves: sea white	29
11	56 – 63	violent storm	exceptionally high waves	37
12	64 +	hurricane	air filled with foam and spray	–

5 Navigation

It is outside the scope of this book to teach navigation. The following three groups of skills should be learnt by intending sea canoeists. Allowances must always be made for the effect of weather and tide.

Group 1

relevant to simple introductory inshore trips in good weather,

1　Interpretation of signs and symbols used on topographical maps. (Information found in the legend on each map and any simple book on map-reading.)
2　Interpretation of signs, symbols and abbreviations used on Admiralty Charts. (Information found in Admiralty booklet number 5011).
3　Knowledge of buoyage systems and rule of the road (see *Reed's Nautical Almanac*).

Group 2

Relevant to more advanced trips where offshore islands are visited and weather conditions are uncertain,

1 Skills as in Group 1.
2 Ability to use an orienteering type compass to calculate magnetic bearing between two given points.
3 Knowledge of how to paddle on the calculated course.
4 Ability to work out position offshore, in good visibility, between two visible marks (page 136).

All this information can be found in most simple books on map and compass work, e.g. *Know the Game – Orienteering.*

Group 3

relevant to advanced trips where long sea passages are involved

1 Detailed knowledge of charts, pilotage and rule of the road.
2 Ability to work out bearings from a chart using parallel rulers and dividers.
3 Ability to use steering compass, suitably fixed to canoe, to steer on accurate course, even in bad weather.
4 Ability to take a magnetic bearing, using a hand held compass, and use on map or chart.
5 Ability to combine these skills to work out a position using direct reckoning.
6 Knowledge of direction-finding instruments.
7 Ability to make use of natural phenomena (e.g. sun, stars) to assist navigation.

Apart from studying relevant books on navigation, it is advised that canoeists who intend undertaking advanced sea trips should receive some more formal instruction in navigation skills, e.g. lectures or correspondence course.

6 Maps, charts and guides

Many national canoe associations (see page 165) have available to members maps, guides and access information. It is advised that canoeists should join their national association or an affiliated canoe club and make use of these facilities.

In addition, the following sources may be useful:

Great Britain

Inland – Ordnance Survey Maps, Southampton, or any large bookshop or stationers.

Sea – Admiralty charts, published by the Hydrographic Department of the Ministry of Defence, Taunton, Somerset. Obtainable from Admiralty agents throughout the British Isles and abroad.

Canada and USA

Inland – topographical maps are available from local stores or by mail from:

Mississippi River (East), Distribution Section, US. Geological Survey, Washington DC 20242.
Mississippi River (West), Distribution Section, US Geological Survey, Federal Center, Denver, Colorado 80225.
Alaska, US Geological Survey, 520 Illinois Street, Fairbanks, Alaska.
Map Distribution Center, Department of Mines and Technical Surveys, Ottawa, Ontario.
Army Corps of Engineers Waterway Maps, US Army Corps of Engineers, Office of the Chief Engineers, Forrestal Building, Washington DC, 20314.

Sea

US Coast and Geodetic Survey, Att, Map Information Service C – 513, Rock Ville, MD 20852.
The Coastguard, 400 7th Street SW, Washington DC 20590.

7 International system of grading of wild-water rivers

These difficulty ratings are currently under review.

Grade 1: easy

Occasional small rapids, waves regular and low. Correct course easy to find, but care is needed with obstacles like pebble banks, protective works and fallen trees.

Grade 2: medium

Fairly frequent rapids, regular waves, easy eddies. Course generally easy to recognise. (On the Continent: easy and medium raft channels.)

Grade 3: difficult

Rapids numerous and with fairly high, irregular waves, broken water, eddies and whirlpools. Course not always easily recognised. (Difficult raft channels.)

Grade 4: very difficult

Long and extended rapids with high irregular waves, difficult broken water, eddies and whirlpools. Course often difficult to recognise. Inspection from the bank advised. (Very difficult raft channels.)

Grade 5: exceedingly difficult

Long unbroken stretches of rapids with difficult and completely irregular broken water, submerged rocks, very fast whirlpools and eddies. Inspection from bank strongly advised.

Grade 6: absolute limit of difficulty

All previously mentioned difficulties increased to the limit of practicability. Cannot be attempted without risk to life.

The grading will increase by one grade if the temperature drops below 50°F.

Individual rapids may have a separate, higher grading than the rest of the river. These can usually be portaged.

Grade 1 and 2 rivers are suitable for beginners, Grade 3 for intermediate paddlers and Grade 4 and above only for very experienced canoeists.

8 First aid

Canoeing may take you out of reach of the usual medical assistance. It is recommended that canoeists undergo a recognized training course on current methods of first aid. Could you cope with the following?

Major

apparent drowning
heart failure
haemorrhage
shock
hypothermia
heat exhaustion
burns
major fractures
bites and stings
poisoning
infection, external or internal

Minor

blisters
cuts
burns
bruises
bites and stings
sea sickness
infection, external or internal

On the average day trip your first aid kit should contain:

2 by 3 inch crepe bandages
1 roll 2 inch gauze bandage
2 large wound dressing pads
2 triangular bandages
1 pack sterile, non stick burn dressing
1 roll waterproof adhesive
1 tube antiseptic cream
1 small bottle antiseptic lotion
12 codeine tablets
12 sea-sickness tablets
12 anti-diarrhoea tablets
sunburn cream
tweezers
scissors

If you intend canoeing in remote areas you should ask your doctor for advice on the type and dosage of suitable painkillers, antibiotics and a suture pack. In some districts a snakebite kit is advised and also plenty of insect repellent.

Prevention is better than cure.

9 Building and repairs in glass-reinforced plastic

Building

Although it is not difficult to build a GRP canoe, it is strongly recommended that initially you work with an experienced canoe-builder. Mistakes could ruin your canoe and the mould, which would be an expensive error. A brief outline of the construction method used follows:

1 Borrow or hire canoe mould.
2 Polish the moulds (deck, hull, cockpit).
3 Apply release agent. Cut the glass mat to shape.
4 Apply gel coat to moulds.
5 Laminate glass mat on deck mould using resin.

6   Laminate mat on hull mould. (Number of laminations is dictated by thickness of glass mat used and the required final weight of the canoe.)
7   Add footrest fitting.
8   Laminate cockpit mould.
9   Trim edges of hull, deck and cockpit.
10   Bolt hull mould to deck mould.
11   Join hull and deck using a glass mat strip and resin on a long handled brush.
12   Release boat from mould.
13   Fit buoyancy blocks.
14   Fit cockpit.

Repairs

Most people should be able to repair holes in GRP canoes. With experience major repairs, including rejoining the two halves of a broken canoe, can be carried out.

1   Dry the damaged area thoroughly.
2   Rub down the area to be patched and several inches around, using a coarse grade glass paper.
3   Cut a piece of mat to fit inside the prepared area. Round off any corners.
4   Mix a small amount of resin with the catalyst.
5   Using a clean paint brush, spread the resin over the prepared area.
6   Place the mat in position. Using the brush, dab the mat until the resin is worked through very thoroughly.
7   Clean the brush.
8   When perfectly hard, rub down the patch with wet and dry glass paper.

Repair kits

1   On a short trip, most repairs can be carried out using adhesive waterproof tape and, if necessary, a piece of polythene.
2   On longer trips, a pack of fibreglass mat, resin, catalyst and knife should be carried, well away from the food, to effect permanent repairs.
3   Some firms produce instant patches, which when exposed to ultraviolet light, make a semi-permanent repair.

In all three cases, the damaged area must be completely dry before the repair starts. This may necessitate the use of heat.

10 Canoeing for the disabled

Many disabled people can take part in canoeing on equal terms with the able-bodied. The only requirements are to be able to swim and be water-confident, have a reasonable sense of balance, to be able to sit up and have the use of both hands and arms.

Some people can use a standard canoe; others may need individual adaptations, usually very simple, to make the canoe fit. Many canoe manufacturers are happy to make these adaptations for the individual.

Wetsuits are recommended as they give good protection against bruises and cold.

If you, or someone you know, are disabled and want to canoe, contact your local canoe club. You may have to convince them of your intent but most will be helpful. If you have problems, contact your National Canoe Association (page 165) or, in Britain, The Sports Council, 70 Brompton Road, London, SW3.

11 British Canoe Manufacturers Association (manufacturers of canoes and/or accessories)

Members

Countries listed in brackets denote those in which the manufacturer has agents.

A.C. Canoe Products (Chester) Ltd, P.O. Box 62, Chester.
Arrowcraft Marine Ltd, 19, Lingfield Close, Great Wyrley, Walsall.
Avoncraft, Burrowfield, Welwyn Garden City, Hertfordshire (*Norway, Sweden, Holland, Belgium, Germany, Canada*).
Canoe Centre (Twickenham) Ltd, 18, Beauchamp Road, Twickenham, Middlesex, (*Norway, Sweden, Denmark, Germany, Luxembourg*).
Cymru Canoes, St. Hilary's Road, Llanrhos, Llandudno, Gwynedd.
Gaybo Ltd, 4, Rosehill, Brighton.
Harishok Ltd, 12A, Jackson Street, Hyde, Cheshire.
Kama Canoes, The Old School, Siddick, Workington, Cumbria.
Lendal Products Ltd, 18–20, Boyd Street, Prestwick, Ayrshire.

McNulty Seaglass Ltd, Victoria Road, South
Shields, Tyne and Wear (*Ireland, Holland,
Sweden, Norway, America, Canada,
Australia*).
Northern Kayaks, Rothbury Industrial Estate,
Rothbury, Northumbria.
P & H Fibreglass Ltd, Old Stanley Colliery,
Station Road, West Hallam, Ilkeston, Derby
(*Germany, Switzerland*).
Trylon Ltd, Wollaston, Northants (*Hong Kong*).
Valley Canoe Products Ltd., Private Road 4,
Colwick Estate, Nottingham (*Sweden,
Norway, Holland, Canada, Australia,
Tasmania, New Zealand, West Germany,
Eire*).
Wild Water Centre, The Mill, Glasshouses,
Pateley Bridge, Harrogate, Yorkshire
(*Australia, Austria, Belgium, Germany,
Switzerland, South Africa, USA*).

Other Canoe/Accessory Manufacturers.

Baron Canoes Ltd, Hatch Moor Trading Estate,
Great Torrington, N. Devon.
Granta Boats Ltd, 23, Great Whyte, Ramsey,
Huntingdon, Cambs.
Ottersports Ltd, Ash Street, Northampton.
Pyranha Mouldings Ltd, Marina Village,
Preston Brook, Runcorn, Cheshire.
Whitewater Sports, 22, Guildford Road,
Woking, Surrey.

12 Suggested further reading

Historical

O.J. Cock, *A Short History of Canoeing in
Britain*, British Canoe Union, 1974
Edwin Tappan Adney and Howard I.
Chapelle, *The Bark Canoes and Skin Boats
of North America*, US Government Printing
Office, Washington DC, 1964

General Canoeing

Brian Skilling, *Canoeing Complete*, revised
edition, Kaye and Ward, 1973
Alan Byde, *Living Canoeing*, Adam and
Charles Black, third edition 1979
Derek Hutchinson, *Sea Canoeing*, Adam and
Charles Black, 1976
R. Steidle, *Wildwater Canoeing*, EP
Publishing, 1977
John R. Ramwell, *Sea Touring*, third edition, 32
Glebe Road, West Perry, Huntingdon,
Cambs, 1978

Kayak Canoeing, Know the Game series, EP
Publishing

Narrative

Mike Jones, *Canoeing Down Everest*, Hodder
and Stoughton, 1979
John MacGregor, *1,000 Miles in the Rob Roy
Canoe*, facsimile, British Canoe Union
Kenneth Brower Holt *The Starship and the
Canoe*, Rinehart and Winston, New York,
1978
J.M. Scott, *Gino Watkins*, Hodder and
Stoughton, 1935 (out of print)

Canoe-Camping

Roy Bearse, *The Canoe Camper's Handbook*,
Winchester Press, New York, 1974
I. Herbert Gordon, *The Canoe Book*,
McGraw-Hill, New York, 1978

(Both these books deal specifically with the
open Canadian Canoe. However, they contain
excellent advice on techniques of canoe
camping and many useful addresses relevant
to Canada and the USA.)

Safety

British Canoe Union Coaching Handbook, sixth
edition, British Canoe Union, 1979
First Aid, authorized manual of St John
Ambulance Association, third Edition, 1972
Jane Renouf and Steward Hulse, *First Aid for
Hill Walkers and Climbers* Penguin, 1978
W.R. Keatinge, *Survival in Cold Water*,
Blackwell, 1969
Corps of Canoe Lifeguards Manual, third
edition, British Canoe Union, 1974

Canoe building and repairs

Alan Byde, *Canoe Building in
Glass-Reinforced Plastic.*, Adam and
Charles Black, 1977
How to Build a Glassfibre Canoe, fifth edition,
Trylon, Thrift Street, Wollaston, Northants,
1979

Weather

A.G. Forsdyke, *The Weather Guide*, Hamlyn,
1969
John Hulbert, *All About Weather*, Carousel,
1973
G.W. While, *Outlook*, Kandy, 1967
F.E. Newing and Richard Bowood *The
Weather*, Ladybird, 1962

Alan Watts, *Instant Weather Forecasting*, Adlard Coles, 1968

Weather Forecasts, Royal Yachting Association, Victoria Way, Woking, Surrey, 1972

Navigation and tides

Peter Johnson, *Yachting World Handbook*, second edition, Stanford Maritime, 1972

G.G. Watkins, *Coastwise Navigation*, second edition, Stanford Maritime, 1972

Ken Duxbury, *Seastate and Tides*, Stanford Maritime, 1977

Arthur N. Strahler, *The Earth Sciences*, Harper and Row, 1963

O.M. Watts, *Reed's Nautical Almanac*, (annual)

J.B. Harley, *Ordnance Survey Maps*, Ordnance Survey, Southampton, 1975

Map Reading, Know the Game series, EP Publishing

Orienteering, Know the Game series, EP Publishing

David Lewis, *The Voyaging Stars*, Collins, 1978

Miscellaneous

Water Sports for the Disabled, The Sports Council, 70 Brompton Road, London SW3

Report of British Kayak Expedition to Nordkapp, Colin Mortlock. Old Fisherbeck, Ambleside, Cumbria.

Index